THIMBLEBERRIES®

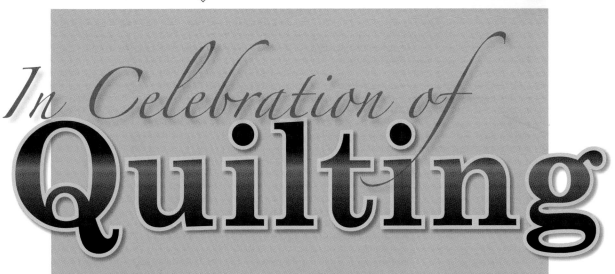

In Celebration of
Quilting

contents

Thimbleberries®
In Celebration of Quilting

Copyright© 2008 by Thimbleberries®
7 North Main Street,
Hutchinson, MN 55350
www.thimbleberries.com
800/587-3944

Editor: Becky Johnston
Book Designer: Brian Shearer
Photographer: Craig Anderson
Technical Writer: Sue Bahr
Technical Illustrator: Lisa Kirchoff
Art Director: Kate Grussing
Thimbleberries® Design Studio

The following manufacturers are licensed to
sell Thimbleberries® products: Thimbleberries®
Rugs (www.colonialmills.com); Thimbleberries®
Quilt Stencils (www.quiltingcreations.com);
Thimbleberries® Sewing Thread (available at
independent quilt shops); and Thimbleberries®
Fabrics (RJR Fabrics available at independent
quilt shops).

On the cover:
"The Log Cabin Quilt featured on the cover
is a recognizable quilt pattern—versatile,
scrappy, historic, traditional and yet
contemporary—and my all-time favorite."
On opposite page:
Several other favorite quilt design elements
including Flying Geese, Pinwheel, Pine Tree
and House, Heart and Stars are staples in
the Thimbleberries Library that inspired the
Thimbleberries Celebration Sampler Quilt
shown opposite and on page 132.

A Season to Plant

16 "The true joy of my business is that
designing involves exactly what I'd
do for a hobby."

A Season to Grow

44 "Gardening has been a large part of my
visual life and its influence is evident
in my designs."

A Season to Harvest

72 "Autumn has always been my
favorite season of the year, with the
crisp scent of cool mornings that
warm to sunny afternoons—just
right for gathering nature's harvest."

A Season to Celebrate

94 "In looking back to what has brought
Thimbleberries to a future bright with
promise, I'm reminded that through all
the years, we didn't just make quilts.
We made history. My contribution is
what quilters around the world call
Thimbleberries."

foreword

My earliest childhood memories are of a home filled with the art of the needle.

Many pleasant hours were spent playing with toys that really worked—from my low-voltage electric iron to the miniature sewing machine shown here. Much of that "practice makes perfect" led to my life-long love for needlework of any kind. We not only sewed, but plied our needles in knit and crochet, embroidery and, of course, quilting.

Growing up surrounded by such simple comforts as embroidered dishtowels, crockery, cookbooks, quilts, rugs, stitcheries, tins and toys, it was only natural that I've not only saved many of the original family keepsakes but collected many similar vintage companion pieces along the way.

From the toys we cherished to the plaid umbrella collection with Lucite® and Bakelite handles, color and pattern have inspired what has become a design-driven business aptly named Thimbleberries®. And it is this heritage that has made it possible for me to plant, grow, harvest and celebrate 20 years of my best in quilting, gardening and decorating. You'll find it all in the pages of this book along with quilting inspirations and a Celebration Sampler Quilt designed to welcome you home. Enjoy!

Lynette Jensen

"I recall to this day the sights, sounds and smells of my childhood home and garden."

Many of the keepsakes I've collected over the years have become treasured reminders of the place we called "home." My mother's dustpan now hangs on the garden house cupboard door and the drying rack proudly displays embroidered feedsack dishtowels—some old, some newly embroidered by a dear friend using antique toweling and vintage embroidery stencils—while my mother's hem marker still stands as a nostalgic reminder of the familiar sound of the click, click, click of pins going into the hem of a dress as we slowly turned, turned, turned.

The quaint plaid puppy pincushion with a tape measure tail and the vintage sewing items displayed in large jars as a form of artwork are a gentle reminder of those who put them to good use making wonderful things that are still in service today. Sewing and making things by hand are a huge part of my background. From my mother and/or my grandmother I learned how to sew, crochet, knit, embroider and weave. For them a necessity—for me a way to express my creativity and later individualize and develop my own decorating style.

Generally, every one of my collections started with a family piece. The variety of textures, colors, shapes and added benefit of being quite utilitarian have given pottery an important place in my home and heart. When I see the pottery bowls and brown pottery jars I'm fondly reminded of my grandmother's special one that always held apple butter. Another jar was used to collect cooking grease that would eventually be a vital ingredient in her homemade soap.

Treasured family cookbooks and a clever recipe card box disguised as a small cardboard stove are pleasant reminders of the dozens of casseroles and desserts with taste-tempting aromas wafting from my mother's kitchen from dawn to dusk.

Vintage tin food containers and picnic baskets are constant reminders of a time when society was not based on everything being disposable. I've always been intrigued by the unique period artwork and the intended long-use as a secondary purpose of an item used for packaging. I continue to put these decorative, but hard-working vintage tins to good use as storage containers since I find them much more interesting than plastic containers.

Even rusty tin picnic baskets artfully spend their final years serving as handy portable planters in my garden.

"I treasure the handiwork of others from an earlier time...I think it is

My favorite Christmas gift began life as an ordinary apple crate. For many evenings my mother secretly painted and trimmed it to be ready for me to discover under the tree on Christmas morning. I had the privilege of finishing what she started. I recall spending hours "decorating" my apple crate doll house (shown above) with assorted scraps of wallpaper and fabric.

To this day my love for houses is evidenced by the vintage pieces I collect— replicas of miniature houses, hand-hooked rugs from wool or assorted fabric strips, and hand-stitched samplers and pictures basically made from thread.

I can't bear to have someone's work go by unappreciated, knowing it was done most likely with little money or expendable free time to make daily life more pleasant and enjoyable.

Many of the houses featured in the mellow colors of the vintage artwork in my growing collection are actually from the era of houses I've lived in over the years.

Most of all, houses of all shapes and sizes are integral to many of the designs I create for Thimbleberries.

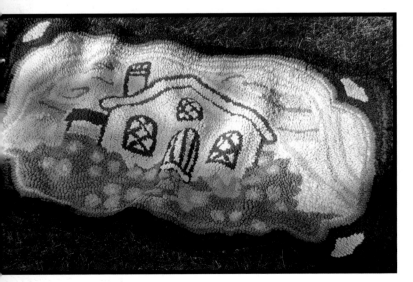

"For me, Thimbleberries came to mean 'the fruit of the thimble.'"

Rubus parviflorus (Thimbleberry) is a species of Rubus, native to western and northern North America, from Alaska east to Ontario and Minnesota, and south to northern Mexico. It grows from sea level in the north, up to 2,500 m in altitude in the south of the range. The plant is said to have given its name to the Thimble Islands in Connecticut, although it is rarely seen in that area of the country.

THIMBLEBERRIES®

The Thimbleberry is a dense shrub up to 2.5 m tall with canes 3–15 mm in diameter, often growing in large clumps along roadsides and in forest clearings. It has no thorns. The leaves are large, soft and fuzzy in texture with five lobes as shown above. The flowers are 2–6 cm in diameter, with five white petals surrounding pale yellow stamens.

It produces a tart edible composite fruit 10–15 mm in diameter, which ripen to a bright red in mid to late summer. Like other raspberries, it is not a true berry, but instead an aggregate fruit of numerous drupelets around a central core; the drupelets may be carefully removed separately from the core when picked, leaving a hollow fruit which bears a resemblance to a thimble, thus the name for the plant. Thimbleberry plants can be propagated most successfully by planting dormant rhizome segments, as well as from seeds or stem cuttings.

Thimbleberry fruits are larger, flatter, and softer than raspberries, and have many small seeds. Because the ripe fruit is so soft (similar to a mulberry), it does not pack or ship well, so thimbleberries are rarely cultivated or sold commercially.

However, wild thimbleberries make an excellent jam that is sold as a local delicacy in some parts of their range, notably in the Keweenaw Peninsula of Upper Michigan.

Thimbleberry jam is easily made by combining equal parts of berries and sugar, boiling the mixture for two minutes, and packing it into jars.

Many of the influences and inspirations for my designs for Thimbleberries are still part of my everyday life. From our home and garden overlooking a bend in the river to my collection of vintage umbrellas that creates a bold collage of color and pattern—infused in the Bakelite and Lucite® handles and complemented by the plaids and stripes of the fashion fabrics of the era— I'm surrounded by simple pleasures of the past and present. Together, they blend beautifully into a distinctive style that encompasses 20 years of my best.

Go confidently in the direction of your dreams. Live the life you've imagined.

—Henry David Thoreau (1817–1842)
Essayist and Philosopher

a season to plant

Growing a business is a lot like planting a garden. It all starts with a few tools and a handful of tiny seeds planted in the proper soil that offer the promise of big, beautiful blooms. If given the right amount of water, sunshine and plenty of loving care along the way, a carefully cultivated garden can be a work of art and afford lasting pleasure. So it is with a business that begins as a mere vision and with great attention to detail, blossoms into an established brand.

For Lynette Jensen, inspirations for designs have come from collecting everything from the unique to the ordinary. Whether antique or recently handcrafted, Lynette's vintage quilt collection has played a key role in the eventual creation of Thimbleberries.

Lynette quickly transitioned beyond collecting quilts to quiltmaking and teaching others at a local fabric store and community education classes through the local school district and, in doing so, discovered her true passion—quilting.

Prairie Pines, the first Thimbleberries pattern, was published in 1988. It was the result of a popular class Lynette taught at a local fabric store.

Countryside Wreaths was first published in 1989 as shown above. The popular design has endured for 19 years and remains a staple of Thimbleberries. See page 122 for an updated version.

Around Town features house motifs that have become Thimbleberries favorites and appear frequently as new groups of patterns are introduced.

It wasn't long after Lynette began making her own quilts using traditional quilt block patterns, that she designed her first template-based pattern inspired by her Minnesota roots and surroundings aptly named *Prairie Pines,* followed by *Countryside Wreaths* and *Around Town.* Twenty years later Lynette is an accomplished quilt and fabric designer who is the best-selling author of dozens of books and patterns with nearly a million copies sold. She has inspired a generation of dedicated quilters to feather their nests with enduring Thimbleberries designs on fabrics, patterns and books available in more than 2,400 independent quilt shops.

In those early years of expressing her creativity through designing patterns for quilting, Lynette discovered that by creating her own line of coordinating prints, solids, and plaids she could get exactly what she needed for her growing collection of pieced patchwork. A successful working relationship with RJR Fashion Fabrics begun in 1993 has resulted in an expansive line of fabrics in a rich palette of colors that literally spans the seasons. Lynette combines traditional quilt patterns of pieced blocks with an appealing array of appliquéd vines, berries, and blossoms. The result is a charming blend of blocks and borders with soft touches of color for a unique style reminiscent of America's more tranquil past.

In recent years, Thimbleberries has grown beyond designs licensed for fabric to other products including books, embroidery designs, calendars, journals, stencils, thread, rugs and a collection of care products including crafter's hand lotion, quilt wash and linen spray.

"The true joy of my business is that designing involves exactly what I'd do for a hobby."

The Prairie Pines Quilt shown here is the original made as a class sampler in 1988. Different fabrics were used for piecing each tree motif with multi-fabrics used for the background. See page 98 for this classic pattern.

Favorite quilt block patterns such as Star & Chain have delighted generations of quilters. Lynette continues to build upon that tradition by offering quilters patterns that utilize new time-saving tools and techniques such as modern rotary cutting along with enduring fabric collections by Thimbleberries.

Star & Chain Quilt

64 x 76-inches

Fabrics and Supplies

1 yard **each** of **5 COORDINATING GOLD** and **GREEN PRINTS** for star and chain blocks

5 yards **BEIGE PRINT** for background

1/2 yard **GREEN PLAID** for chain blocks

3/4 yard **GREEN PLAID** for binding (cut on the bias)

4 yards for backing

quilt batting, at least 70 x 82-inches

Before beginning this project, read through **Getting Started** on page 154

STAR BLOCKS
Makes 6 blocks using **each GOLD** and **GREEN PRINT** (30 total)

Cutting
From **each GOLD** and **GREEN PRINT**:
- Cut 6, 4-1/2-inch squares (30 total)
- Cut 3, 2-1/2 x 42-inch strips. From the strips cut:
  48, 2-1/2-inch squares. (240 total)

From **BEIGE PRINT**:
- Cut 21, 2-1/2 x 42-inch strips. From the strips cut:
  120, 2-1/2 x 4-1/2-inch rectangles
  120, 2-1/2-inch squares

Piecing
Step 1 With right sides together, position a 2-1/2-inch **GOLD** or **GREEN** square on the corner of a 2-1/2 x 4-1/2-inch **BEIGE** rectangle. Draw a diagonal line on the square and stitch on the line. Trim the seam allowance to 1/4-inch; press. Repeat this process at the opposite corner of the rectangle.

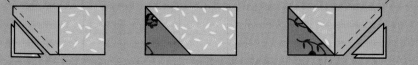

Make 24 Star point units using each **GOLD** and **GREEN** fabric

Step 2 Sew coordinating star point units to the top/bottom edges of each 4-1/2-inch coordinating square; press. Sew 2-1/2-inch **BEIGE** squares to both side edges of the remaining star point units; press. Sew the units to the side edges of each coordinating block; press. <u>At this point each star block should measure 8-1/2-inches square.</u>

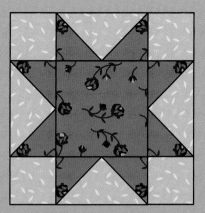

Make 6 star blocks from
GOLD and **GREEN** fabric

CHAIN BLOCK UNITS
Makes 24 units using each **GOLD** and **GREEN PRINT** (120 total)
Makes 22 units using **GREEN PLAID**

Cutting
From each **GOLD** and **GREEN PRINT**:
• Cut 6, 2-1/2 x 42-inch strips from each fabric. From each of the strips cut:
  48, 2-1/2 x 4-1/2-inch rectangles (240 total)

From **BEIGE PRINT**:
• Cut 36, 2-1/2 x 42-inch strips. From the strips cut:
  568, 2-1/2-inch squares

From **GREEN PLAID**:
• Cut 5, 2-1/2 x 42-inch strips. From the strips cut:
  44, 2-1/2 x 4-1/2-inch rectangles

Piecing
Step 1 With right sides together, position a 2-1/2-inch **BEIGE** square on the corner of a 2-1/2 x 4-1/2-inch **GOLD** or **GREEN** rectangle. Draw a diagonal line on the square; stitch, trim, and press. Repeat this process at the opposite corner of the rectangle referring to the diagram for the stitching direction.

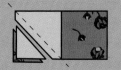   

Make 24 chain block units
using each **GOLD** and
GREEN fabric

Step 2 Repeat Step 1 reversing the direction of the stitching lines.

Make 24 chain block
units using each **GOLD**
and **GREEN** fabric

Step 3 Sew the Step 1 and Step 2 units together in pairs to make chain blocks; press.

Make 24 chain blocks using each
GOLD and **GREEN** fabric

Step 4 With right sides together, position a 2-1/2-inch **BEIGE** square on the corner of a 2-1/2 x 4-1/2-inch **GREEN PLAID** rectangle. Draw a diagonal line on the square; stitch, trim, and press. Repeat this process at the opposite corner of the rectangle referring to the diagram for the stitching direction.

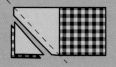  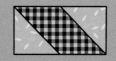

Make 22 chain block units
using **GREEN PLAID**

Step 5 Repeat Step 4 reversing the direction of the stitching lines.

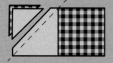  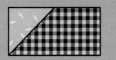 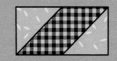

Make 22 chain block units
using **GREEN PLAID**

Step 6 Sew the Step 4 and Step 5 units together in pairs to make chain blocks; press.

Make 22 chain blocks using
GREEN PLAID

QUILT CENTER

Cutting
From **BEIGE PRINT**:
• Cut 5, 4-1/2 x 42-inch strips. From the strips cut: 42, 4-1/2-inch squares.

Quilt Center Assembly
Step 1 For the top/bottom chain block rows, sew the **GREEN PLAID** and **GOLD/GREEN** units together in pairs; press. Referring to page 31 for placement, sew the chain block units and 4-1/2-inch **BEIGE** squares together; press. At this point the top/bottom chain block rows should measure 4-1/2 x 56-1/2-inches. Label the top/bottom chain block rows and set aside.

Make 1 top chain block row

Make 1 bottom chain block row

Step 2 For the side chain block rows, sew the remaining **GREEN PLAID** units and the **GOLD/GREEN** units together in pairs; press. Sew the chain block units and 4-1/2-inch **BEIGE** squares together; press. At this point the side chain block rows should measure 4-1/2 x 76-1/2-inches. Label the right and left side chain block rows and set aside.

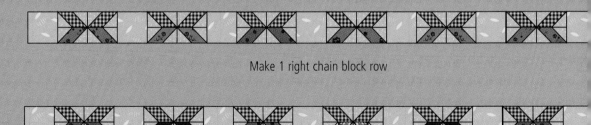

Make 1 right chain block row

Make 1 left chain block row

Step 3 Referring to the quilt assembly diagram for placement, lay out the star blocks and the remaining coordinating chain units. Sew the chain units together in pairs; press. Make 49 chain blocks. Position the chain blocks back in place with the star blocks.

Quilt Assembly Diagram

Step 4 Sew the star blocks and the chain blocks together in 6 horizontal rows. Press the seam allowances toward the star blocks. At this point each star/chain block row should measure 8-1/2 x 56-1/2-inches.

Step 5 Sew the remaining chain blocks and 4-1/2-inch **BEIGE** squares together in 5 horizontal rows. Press the seam allowances toward the squares. At this point each chain block row should measure 4-1/2 x 56-1/2-inches.

Step 6 Referring to the quilt assembly diagram for placement, sew the star block rows and the chain block rows together; press.

Step 7 Sew the Step 1 top/bottom chain block rows to the quilt center; press.

Step 8 Sew the Step 2 right/left chain block rows to the quilt center; press. At this point the quilt top should measure 64-1/2 x 76-1/2-inches.

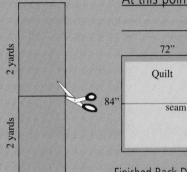

Finished Back Diagram

PUTTING IT ALL TOGETHER

Cut the 4 yard length of backing fabric in half crosswise to make 2, 2 yard lengths. Refer to **Finishing the Quilt** on page 156 for complete instructions.

TB 18 - 11" Lady Slipper

Quilting Suggestions:
- Center **TB18 - 11" Lady Slipper** on each of the star/chain blocks
- Meander the **GREEN PLAID/BEIGE** outer edge

THIMBLEBERRIES quilt stencils by Quilting Creations International are available at your local quilt shop or visit www.quiltingcreations.com.

BINDING

Cutting
From **GREEN PLAID**:
- Cut enough 2-3/4-inch wide **bias** strips to make a 290-inch long strip.

Sew the binding to the quilt using a 3/8-inch seam allowance. This measurement will produce a 1/2-inch wide finished double binding. Refer to page 156 for **Binding** and **Diagonal Piecing** instructions.

Star & Chain Quilt
64 x 76-inches

Yo-Yo Table Topper

15 x 30-inches

Fabrics and Supplies

1/4 yard **BEIGE FLORAL** for back of squares
1 yard **LARGE BLUE FLORAL** for blocks and outer border yo-yos
3/8 yard **RED/GREEN PLAID** for binding (cut on the bias)
1/2 yard **ROSE FLORAL** for lattice and inner border yo-yos
1/2 yard **GREEN PRINT** for middle border yo-yos
quilt batting, at least 7 x 20-inches
template material for yo-yos (posterboard, manila folder)
Note: We used Mountain Mist® Gold-Fuse, baste free fusible cotton
polyester batting

Before beginning this project, read through **Getting Started** on page 154.

BLOCKS

Cutting
From **LARGE BLUE FLORAL**:
• Cut 1, 6 x 42-inch strip. From the strip cut:
  3, 6-inch squares

From **BEIGE FLORAL**:
• Cut 1, 6 x 42-inch strip. From the strip cut:
  3, 6-inch backing squares

From batting:
• Cut 3, 6-inch squares

From **RED/GREEN PLAID**:
• Cut enough 2-1/2-inch wide **bias** strips to make a 90-inch long strip.

Refer to **Diagonal Piecing** instructions on page 156 to piece the strips
together.

Assembly
Step 1 With right sides facing out, layer a 6-inch **LARGE BLUE FLORAL**
  square, batting square, and **BEIGE FLORAL** backing square. Referring to
  manufacturer's instructions, fuse the layers together with baste free fusible
  batting or hand baste the layers together.

Make 3 Blocks

Step 2 Using the 2-1/2-inch wide **RED/GREEN PLAID** binding strip, bind the prepared block. Sew the binding to the block using a 1/4-inch seam allowance. This measurement will produce a 1/4-inch wide finished double binding. Refer to **Binding** on page 156 for complete instructions. At this point each finished block should measure 6-inches square.

YO-YO LATTICE and BORDERS

Step 1 Trace the yo-yo pattern onto template material; cut out.

Step 2 Trace around the template on the wrong side of the designated fabrics. Trace 48 **ROSE FLORAL** yo-yos for lattice and inner border, trace 48 **GREEN** yo-yos for middle border, and trace 56 **LARGE BLUE FLORAL** yo-yos for outer border.

Yo-yo Circle

Cut 48 **Rose Floral** yo-yos
Cut 48 **Green Print** yo-yos
Cut 56 **Large Blue Floral** yo-yos

Note: The finished yo-yos should measure 1-1/2-inches in diameter so they will "fit" the 6-inch square finished blocks.

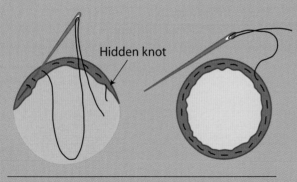

Hidden knot

Step 3 Holding the circle wrong side up in your hand, turn the edges of the circle over to the wrong side of the fabric a scant 1/8-inch. Use one strand of quilting thread to make running stitches close to the fold. Make the stitches approximately 1/4-inch long and 1/4-inch apart. If the running stitches are made too close together, it will be difficult to pull up the stitches to make a nice tight hole in the center of the yo-yo.

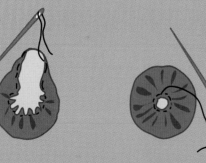

Step 4 The yo-yo is formed when you pull up the gathering thread so the circle is gathered on the right side leaving a small hole in the middle. Pull the thread tight; knot and clip the threads close to the fabric. The backside of the yo-yo will be flat. At this point the finished yo-yo should measure 1-1/2-inches in diameter.

Step 5 Repeat to make the remaining yo-yos. Take care to keep the seam allowances of each circle the same size so each yo-yo will measure 1-1/2-inches in diameter.

Step 6 Referring to the table topper photograph on page 32, lay the yo-yos and finished blocks on a flat surface. Whipstitch the edges of 4 of the **ROSE FLORAL** yo-yos together to make a lattice strip. To sew the yo-yos together, hold the yo-yos with gathered sides together and whipstitch a 1/8-inch section. Make a secure knot and clip the threads. Open this unit flat, and add another yo-yo to the opposite side. Continue in this manner to make a row of 4 yo-yos. The yo-yo lattice strip should measure 6-inches long. Make a total of 2 lattice strips and 2 top/bottom borders. Sew the lattice strips and the finished blocks together with whipstitches. Sew the top/bottom inner border strips in place.

Step 7 Sew the side inner border **ROSE FLORAL** yo-yos to the table topper center in the same manner. There should be 16 yo-yos in each side border.

Step 8 Continue adding the middle border **GREEN** yo-yos and the outer border **LARGE BLUE FLORAL** yo-yos.

The mug mat and plant mat shown at right are charming examples of small yo-yo projects.

Child's Play is an enduring favorite pattern Lynette designed for Thimbleberries that is a light-hearted reminder of a bygone era. Just for "show," the bed ensemble was photographed in Lynette's garden.

Child's Play Quilt

74 x 86-inches

Fabrics and Supplies

2/3 yard **LIGHT RED PRINT** for hourglass units
2/3 yard **GREEN DOT** for hourglass units
2/3 yard **YELLOW PRINT** for hourglass units
2/3 yard **YELLOW/BLUE PRINT** for
  hourglass units
1-7/8 yards **CREAM PRINT** for blocks
  and dogtooth background
2-1/3 yards **DARK BLUE PRINT** for lattice post
  squares and outer border
1-1/4 yards **ROSE PRINT** for inner, middle,
  and dogtooth borders
1/2 yard **LIGHT BLUE PRINT** for middle border
  and corner squares
3/4 yard **ROSE PRINT** for binding
5-1/4 yards for backing
quilt batting, at least 80 x 92-inches

Before beginning this project, read through
Getting Started on page 154.

HOURGLASS UNITS for LATTICE STRIP SECTIONS
Makes 98 blocks

Cutting
From **LIGHT RED PRINT**:
• Cut 4, 5-1/4 x 42-inch strips. From the strips cut:
  25, 5-1/4-inch squares. Cut the squares diagonally into quarters to make
  100 triangles. You will be using only 98 triangles.

From **GREEN DOT**:
• Cut 4, 5-1/4 x 42-inch strips. From the strips cut:
  25, 5-1/4-inch squares. Cut the squares diagonally into quarters to make
  100 triangles. You will be using only 98 triangles.

From **YELLOW PRINT**:
• Cut 4, 5-1/4 x 42-inch strips. From the strips cut:
  25, 5-1/4-inch squares. Cut the squares diagonally into quarters to make
  100 triangles. You will be using only 98 triangles.

From **YELLOW/BLUE PRINT**:
• Cut 4, 5-1/4 x 42-inch strips. From the strips cut:
  25, 5-1/4-inch squares. Cut the squares diagonally into quarters to make
  100 triangles. You will be using only 98 triangles.

Piecing
Step 1 Layer a **LIGHT RED** triangle on a **GREEN DOT** triangle. Stitch
along the bias edge being careful not to stretch the triangles. Press the
seam allowance toward the **LIGHT RED** triangle. Repeat for the remaining
LIGHT RED and **GREEN DOT** triangles. Be sure you sew along the same
bias edge of each triangle set.

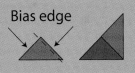

Bias edge

Make 98 triangle units

Step 2 Layer a **YELLOW** triangle on a **YELLOW/BLUE PRINT** triangle. Stitch
along the bias edge; press the seam allowance toward the **YELLOW** triangle.
Repeat for the remaining **YELLOW** and **YELLOW/BLUE PRINT** triangles.

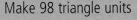

Bias edge

Make 98 triangle units

Step 3 Sew together the Step 1 and Step 2 triangle units in pairs; press.
At this point each hourglass unit should measure 4-1/2-inches square.

Make 98 hourglass units

Step 4 Referring to the diagrams, sew the hourglass units together in pairs
to make the lattice strip sections; press. At this point each lattice strip
section should measure 4-1/2 x 8-1/2-inches.

Make 24
A lattice strip sections

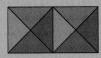

Make 25
B lattice strip sections

QUILT CENTER

Cutting
From **CREAM PRINT:**
- Cut 5, 8-1/2 x 42-inch strips. From the strips cut:
  20, 8-1/2-inch squares

From **DARK BLUE PRINT**:
- Cut 4, 4-1/2 x 42-inch strips. From the strips cut:
  30, 4-1/2-inch lattice post squares

Quilt Center Assembly
Step 1 Sew 4 of the A lattice strip sections and 5 of the 4-1/2-inch **DARK BLUE** lattice post squares together. Press the seam allowances toward the lattice posts. At this point each lattice strip should measure 4-1/2 x 52-1/2-inches.

Make 6 lattice strips

Step 2 Sew 5 of the B lattice strip sections and 4 of the 8-1/2-inch **CREAM** squares together. Press the seam allowances toward the squares. At this point each block row should measure 8-1/2 x 52-1/2-inches.

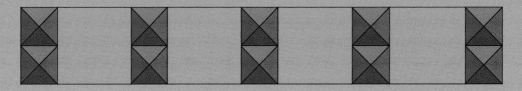

Make 5 block rows

Step 3 Referring to the quilt diagram on page 43, pin the block rows and lattice strips together at the block intersections. Sew the strips together; press. At this point the quilt center should measure 52-1/2 x 64-1/2-inches.

BORDERS

Note: The yardage given allows for the border strips to be cut on the crosswise grain. Diagonally piece the strips as needed, referring to page 156 for **Diagonal Piecing** instructions. Read through **Borders** on page 155 for complete instructions.

Cutting
From **ROSE PRINT**:
- Cut 7, 1-1/2 x 42-inch inner border strips
- Cut 7 more 1-1/2 x 42-inch middle border strips
- Cut 7, 2-1/2 x 42-inch strips. From the strips cut:
  62, 2-1/2 x 4-1/2-inch rectangles

From **LIGHT BLUE PRINT**:
- Cut 7, 1-1/2 x 42-inch middle border strips
- Cut 4, 2-1/2-inch corner squares

From **CREAM PRINT**:
- Cut 8, 2-1/2 x 42-inch strips. From the strips cut:
  124, 2-1/2-inch squares

From **DARK BLUE PRINT**:
- Cut 9, 6-1/2 x 42-inch outer border strips

Assembling and Attaching the Borders
Step 1 Attach the 1-1/2-inch wide **ROSE** inner border strips.

Step 2 Attach the 1-1/2-inch wide **LIGHT BLUE** middle border strips. At this point the quilt center should measure 56-1/2 x 68-1/2-inches.

Step 3 Position a 2-1/2-inch **CREAM** square on the corner of a 2-1/2 x 4-1/2-inch **ROSE** rectangle. Draw a diagonal line on the square and stitch on the line. Trim the seam allowance to 1/4-inch; press. Repeat this process at the opposite corner of the rectangle.

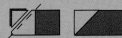

Make 62
dogtooth units

Step 4 For the top/bottom dogtooth borders, sew 14 dogtooth units together; press. At this point each border strip should measure 2-1/2 x 56-1/2-inches. Sew the border strips to the quilt; press.

Step 5 For the side dogtooth borders, sew 17 dogtooth units together; press. Sew the 2-1/2-inch **LIGHT BLUE** corner squares to both ends of the borders; press. Make 2 borders. At this point each border strip should measure 2-1/2 x 72-1/2-inches. Sew the border strips to the quilt; press.

Finished Back Diagram measurements: 42", 2-5/8 yards, 2-5/8 yards, 84", 94", Quilt, seam

Finished Back
Diagram

Step 6 Attach the 1-1/2-inch wide **ROSE** middle border strips.

Step 7 Attach the 6-1/2-inch wide **DARK BLUE** outer border strips.

PUTTING IT ALL TOGETHER

Cut the 5-1/4 yard length of backing fabric in half crosswise to make 2, 2-5/8 yard lengths. Refer to **Finishing the Quilt** on page 156 for complete instructions.

Quilting Suggestions:
- **CREAM** squares - **TB50 - 7-1/2" Heart Loop**
- **DARK BLUE** lattice post squares - **TB23 - 5" Floral Burst** (center only)
- Lattice segments - meander
- **ROSE** and **MEDIUM BLUE** inner borders, quilt as one border - **TB30 - 1-1/2" Beadwork**
- **CREAM** dogtooth border - stipple
- **ROSE** middle border - in-the-ditch
- **DARK BLUE** outer border - **TB37 - 5" Pansy Vine**

TB 50 - 7-1/2"   Heart Loop

TB 23 - 5"   Floral Burst

TB 30 - 1-1/2" Beadwork

TB 37 - 5"   Pansy Vine

THIMBLEBERRIES quilt stencils by Quilting Creations International are available at your local quilt shop or visit www.quiltingcreations.com.

BINDING

Cutting
From **ROSE PRINT**:
- Cut 9, 2-3/4 x 42-inch strips

Sew the binding to the quilt using a 3/8-inch seam allowance. This measurement will produce a 1/2-inch wide finished double binding. Refer to page 156 for **Binding** and **Diagonal Piecing** instructions.

Child's Play Quilt
74 x 86-inches

a season to grow

Nurturing an emerging brand from its humble beginnings as simply a small pattern company to gaining recognition as an internationally-known design source requires patience as well as a commitment to quality that spans the years. Building on new traditions in quilting and expanding beyond that market to new horizons in design has made the name Thimbleberries synonymous with excellence—pure and simple.

"Gardening has been a large part of my visual life and its influence is evident in my designs."

For more than 15 years Neil and Lynette have lived in a restored 1930s classic Colonial situated at the top of a hill that overlooks a bend in the meandering Crow River. Over time, Lynette has transformed the acre surrounding their home with a series of terraced gardens planned to blossom and bloom abundantly from early spring to autumn's first frost.

Old-fashioned favorites such as rhubarb and bushes laden with hydrangeas are at home with towering trees, shrubs and perennials all blended to visual perfection.

In recent years, a garden house was built on site using shingles from the restored Colonial for a unified effect. It offers a practical place for potting and parking not-so-new tools with an interesting patina that even influences Lynette's color palette.

Lynette enjoys the challenge of finding new uses for old things, especially those handmade from wood and other natural materials. In her home, office and garden, painted wooden benches bought at a good price (in addition to those made by her father) are hard at work as side and end tables, extra seating, and even stacked against the wall as a shelving unit to be used as storage for quilts, books, pottery, garden pots and assorted odds and ends.

Sturdy wooden boxes once used to hold carpenter's tools now offer a quick fix for keeping quilter's rulers and other not-so-easy-to-store items collected and close at hand. When used outdoors for floral and greenery displays, a rustic weathered carpenter's tool box is perfectly at home.

"I can always find another use for benches and tool boxes—whether stacked for shelves or simply arranged as a composition of interest."

One Log Cabin pattern pieced in four colorways is proof positive of why this traditional quilt block has been a forever-favorite of quilters who relish the opportunity to slash their stash. It doesn't take long to empty the scrap bag of the bits and pieces of fabric required for the 80 blocks in this generously-sized Log Cabin Quilt.

The Log Cabin Quilt is shown here with an optional 8-inch border. Please refer to page 56 for instructions.

Log Cabin Quilt

64 x 80-inches

Fabrics and Supplies

1/2 yard **RED PRINT** for center squares
3/8 yard each of **18 ASSORTED GREEN PRINTS** for
   log cabin strips
5/8 yard each of **7 ASSORTED BEIGE PRINTS** for log cabin strips
3/4 yard **GREEN DIAGONAL PRINT** for binding
4 yards for backing
quilt batting, at least 70 x 84-inches

Before beginning this project, read through **Getting Started** on page 154.

LOG CABIN BLOCKS
Makes 80 blocks

Cutting
From **RED PRINT:**
- Cut 5, 2-1/2 x 42-inch strips. From the strips cut:
  80, 2-1/2-inch center squares

From **each** of the **18 GREEN PRINTS:**
- Cut 5, 1-1/2 x 42-inch strips

From **each** of the **7 BEIGE PRINTS:**
- Cut 12, 1-1/2 x 42-inch strips

Piecing
Note: You may vary the position of the **BEIGE** fabrics from block to block or place them in the same position in each block. The same is true of the **GREEN** fabrics. The fabric strips in the quilt shown were varied to get a scrappy look. Follow Steps 1 through 5 to piece each of the 80 log cabin blocks.

Step 1 Sew a 1-1/2-inch wide **BEIGE** strip to a 2-1/2-inch **RED** square. Press the seam allowance toward the strip. Trim the strip even with the edges of the center square creating a two-piece unit.

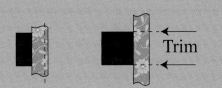

Trim

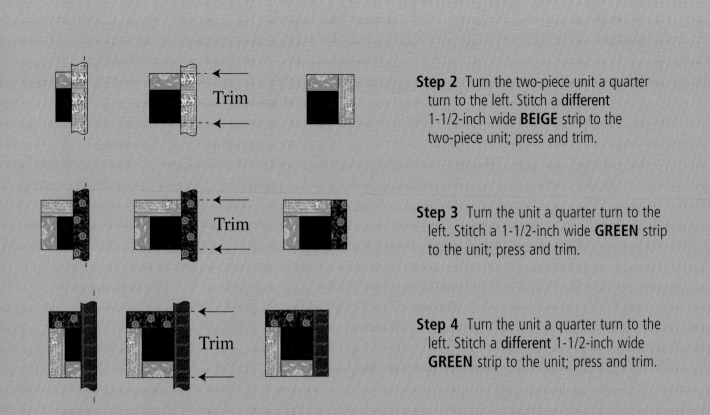

Step 2 Turn the two-piece unit a quarter turn to the left. Stitch a **different** 1-1/2-inch wide **BEIGE** strip to the two-piece unit; press and trim.

Step 3 Turn the unit a quarter turn to the left. Stitch a 1-1/2-inch wide **GREEN** strip to the unit; press and trim.

Step 4 Turn the unit a quarter turn to the left. Stitch a **different** 1-1/2-inch wide **GREEN** strip to the unit; press and trim.

Make 80

Step 5 Referring to the block diagram, continue this process by adding 1-1/2-inch wide strips, alternating **BEIGE** and **GREEN** strips to complete the log cabin block. Press each seam allowance toward the strip just added and trim each strip before adding the next. Each log cabin block should measure 8-1/2-inches square when complete. Adjust the seam allowances if needed.

QUILT CENTER

Step 1 Referring to the quilt diagram for block placement, sew the log cabin blocks together in 10 rows of 8 blocks each. Press the seam allowances in alternating directions by rows so the seams will fit snugly together with less bulk.

Step 2 Pin the rows at the block intersections; sew the rows together and press. At this point the quilt center should measure 64-1/2 x 80-1/2-inches.

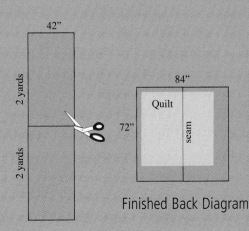

Finished Back Diagram

PUTTING IT ALL TOGETHER

Cut the 4 yard length of backing fabric in half crosswise to make 2, 2 yard lengths. Refer to **Finishing the Quilt** on page 156 for complete instructions. Our quilt was meandered.

BINDING

Cutting
From **GREEN DIAGONAL PRINT:**
• Cut 8, 2-3/4 x 42-inch strips

Sew the binding to the quilt using a 3/8-inch seam allowance. This measurement will produce a 1/2-inch wide finished double binding. Refer to page 156 for **Binding** and **Diagonal Piecing** instructions.

Log Cabin Quilt
64 x 80-inches

Log Cabin Quilt with Border

80 x 96-inches

Fabrics and Supplies

1/2 yard **RED PRINT** for center squares
3/8 yard **each** of **18 ASSORTED DARK PRINTS** for log cabin strips
5/8 yard **each** of **7 ASSORTED BEIGE PRINTS** for log cabin strips
2-3/4 yards **RED FLORAL** for border (cut on the lengthwise grain)
3/4 yard **GREEN PRINT** for binding
7-1/8 yards for backing
quilt batting, at least 86 x 102-inches
Before beginning this project, read through **Getting Started** on page 154.

LOG CABIN BLOCKS
Makes 80 blocks - Refer to **Log Cabin Quilt** pages 53–54 for Cutting and Piecing the log cabin blocks.

Make 80

BORDER

Note: The yardage given allows for the wide outer border strips to be cut on the lengthwise grain (a couple extra inches are allowed for trimming). Cutting the wide border strips lengthwise will eliminate the need for piecing. Read through **Borders** on page 155 for general instructions on adding borders.

Cutting
From **RED FLORAL** (cut on the lengthwise grain):
•Cut 2, 8-1/2 x 99-inch side border strips
•Cut 2, 8-1/2 x 70-inch top/bottom border strips

Attaching the Border
Step 1 Attach the 8-1/2 x 70-inch **RED FLORAL** top/bottom border strips.

Step 2 Attach the 8-1/2 x 99-inch **RED FLORAL** side border strips.

PUTTING IT ALL TOGETHER
Cut the 7-1/8 yard length of backing fabric in thirds crosswise to make 3, 2-3/8 yard lengths. Refer to **Finishing the Quilt** on page 156 for complete instructions.

BINDING

Cutting
From **GREEN PRINT:**
- Cut 9, 2-3/4 x 42-inch strips

Sew the binding to the quilt using a 3/8-inch seam allowance. This measurement will produce a 1/2-inch wide finished double binding. Refer to page 156 for **Binding** and **Diagonal Piecing** instructions.

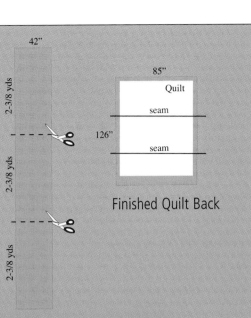

Finished Quilt Back

Log Cabin with Border
80 x 96-inches

Log Cabin Pillow

16-inches square, without ruffle

MAKE A RUFFLED PILLOW USING A 16-INCH QUILT BLOCK

Step 1 Referring to pages 53–54, make 4 log cabin blocks. Sew the log cabin blocks together to make the pillow top; press. <u>At this point, the pillow top should measure 16-1/2 inches square.</u> Layer the pillow top, battting and lining. Quilt as desired.

Step 2 Cut 4, 3 x 44-inch ruffle strips. Diagonally piece the 3-inch wide strips together to make a continuous ruffle strip, referring to page 156 for **Diagonal Piecing** instructions.

Step 3 Fold the strip in half lengthwise, wrong sides together; press. Divide the ruffle strip into 4 equal segments; mark the quarter points with safety pins.

Step 4 To gather the ruffle, position a heavyweight thread 1/4-inch from the raw edges of the folded ruffle strip. You will need a length of thread 160-inches long. Secure one end of the thread by stitching across it. Zigzag stitch over the thread taking care not to sew through it.

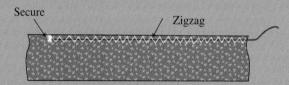

Secure   Zigzag

Step 5 Divide the edges of the pillow top into 4 equal segments; mark the quarter points with safety pins. With right sides together, pin the ruffle to the pillow top, matching the quarter points. Pull up the gathering stitches until the ruffle fits the pillow top, taking care to allow extra fullness in the ruffle at each corner. Machine baste the ruffle to the pillow front, using a 1/4-inch seam allowance.

Step 6 Cut 2, 16-1/2 x 22-inch rectangles for pillow back.

Step 7 With wrong sides together, fold the 16-1/2 x 22-inch rectangles in half to make 2, 11 x 16-1/2-inch double-thick pillow back pieces. Overlap the 2 folded edges so the pillow back measures 16-1/2-inches square; pin. Stitch around the entire piece to create a single pillow back, using a scant 1/4-inch seam allowance.

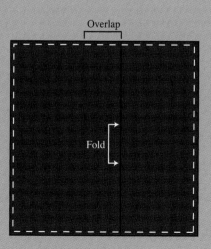

Overlap

Fold

Step 8 With right sides together, layer the pillow back and the pillow top; pin. The ruffle will be sandwiched between the 2 layers and turned toward the center of the pillow at this time. Stitch around the outside edges using a 3/8-inch seam allowance.

Step 9 Turn the pillow right side out, insert a 16-inch square pillow form through the back opening, and fluff up the ruffle.

"From the invitations to the decorations and food for the picnic, everything you need is right in your own backyard. "

Enjoy the fruit of your labors and celebrate summer—right in your own backyard. Decorating is easy when you're surrounded by floral abundance. So now is the time to invite friends and family over for a garden party get-together. Share your good taste with simple fare fresh from your garden.

While your garden is at its peak, treat everyone to a tour and light refreshments such as rhubarb picnic punch (recipe on following page). Start with an invitation that spells out the day and time when you'd like to begin your garden tour. Create your own, or personalize a purchased invitation with a small digital photo of a favorite summer bloom.

Rhubarb Picnic

Ingredients

12 cups rhubarb, sliced

6 quarts water

1 6-oz. can frozen orange juice (undiluted)

3 cups sugar (this may be cut back to 2 cups for a
punch that is not quite as sweet)

1 quart 7-Up® or club soda (again, club soda
would not be quite as sweet, but very refreshing)

Punch

Instructions:

Boil the rhubarb and water together until rhubarb is very soft and falls apart; strain. Add the orange juice, lemonade, and sugar to the strained liquid; mix together until the sugar is dissolved. Add soda just before serving. Serves 8–10.

Paint Box Stars Quilt

94 x 108-inches

Fabrics and Supplies

1/2 yard each of 5 **ASSORTED GOLD PRINTS** for star units
(or 2 yards total of 1 Gold Print)
1 yard each of **5 ASSORTED BEIGE PRINTS** for pieced blocks
(or 4 yards total of 1 Beige Print)
2-5/8 yards **DARK BLUE PRINT** for pieced blocks
1/3 yard **GOLD PRINT** for lattice posts
2-1/4 yards **RED PRINT** for lattice pieces and middle border
3-3/4 yards **BLUE FLORAL** for inner border and
outer border (cut on the lengthwise grain)
1 yard **RED PRINT** for binding
8-1/4 yards for backing
quilt batting, at least 100 x 114-inches

PIECED BLOCKS

Note: Coordinate each **GOLD PRINT** with a **BEIGE PRINT** to make 6
star units. The same **BEIGE PRINT** will be used to complete each of the 6
pieced blocks.

Makes 6 blocks using each **GOLD/BEIGE/DARK BLUE** combination for a
total of 30 pieced blocks.

Cutting

From **each** of the **5 ASSORTED GOLD PRINTS**:
- Cut 1, 4-1/2 x 42-inch strip. From the strip cut:
  6, 4-1/2-inch squares
- Cut 3, 2-1/2 x 42-inch strips. From the strips cut:
  48, 2-1/2-inch squares

From **each** of the **5 ASSORTED BEIGE PRINTS**:
- Cut 11, 2-1/2 x 42-inch strips. From the strips cut:
  24, 2-1/2 x 4-1/2-inch rectangles
  120, 2-1/2-inch squares

From **DARK BLUE PRINT**:
- Cut 35, 2-1/2 x 42-inch strips. From the strips cut:
  240, 2-1/2 x 4-1/2-inch rectangles
  120, 2-1/2-inch squares

Piecing

Step 1 Position a 2-1/2-inch **GOLD** square on the corner of a coordinating 2-1/2 x 4-1/2-inch **BEIGE** rectangle. Draw a diagonal line on the square and stitch on the line. Trim the seam allowance to 1/4-inch; press. Repeat this process at the opposite corner of the rectangle. <u>At this point each star point unit should measure 2-1/2 x 4-1/2-inches.</u>

Make 24 star point units
using each **GOLD/BEIGE**
combination

Make 6 star units using
each **GOLD/BEIGE** combination

Step 2 Sew star point units to the top/bottom edges of a coordinating 4-1/2-inch **GOLD** square; press. Sew coordinating 2-1/2-inch **BEIGE** squares to the remaining Step 1 units; press. Sew the units to the side edges of the square; press. <u>At this point each star unit should measure 8-1/2-inches square.</u>

Step 3 Position a coordinating 2-1/2-inch **BEIGE** square on the corner of a 2-1/2 x 4-1/2-inch **DARK BLUE** rectangle. Draw a diagonal line on the square; stitch, trim, and press. Repeat this process at the opposite corner of the rectangle. <u>At this point each unit should measure 2-1/2 x 4-1/2-inches.</u>

Make 240 units

Step 4 Sew the Step 3 units together in pairs; press. <u>At this point each unit should measure 2-1/2 x 8-1/2-inches.</u>

Make 120 units

Step 5 Sew Step 4 units to the top/bottom edges of a star unit; press. Sew 2-1/2-inch **DARK BLUE** squares to the remaining Step 4 units; press. Sew the units to the side edges of the star unit; press. <u>At this point each pieced block should measure 12-1/2-inches square.</u>

Make 30 pieced blocks

QUILT CENTER

Cutting
From **RED PRINT:**
- Cut 24, 2-1/2 x 42-inch strips. From the strips cut:
  71, 2-1/2 x 12-1/2-inch lattice pieces

From **GOLD PRINT:**
- Cut 3, 2-1/2 x 42-inch strips. From the strips cut:
  42, 2-1/2-inch lattice post squares

Quilt Center Assembly
Step 1 Lay out the pieced blocks and the 2-1/2 x 12-1/2-inch **RED** lattice pieces. Sew together 5 of the pieced blocks and 6 of the **RED** lattice pieces. Press the seam allowances toward the lattice pieces. Make 6 block rows. At this point each block row should measure 12-1/2 x 72-1/2-inches.

Make 6 block rows

Step 2 Sew together 5 of the **RED** lattice pieces and 6 of the 2-1/2-inch **GOLD** lattice posts. Press the seam allowances toward the lattice pieces. Make 7 lattice strips. At this point each lattice strip should measure 2-1/2 x 72-1/2-inches.

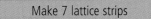

Make 7 lattice strips

Step 3 Referring to the quilt center diagram on page 68, pin the block rows and lattice strips together. Sew the rows together; press. At this point the quilt center should measure 72-1/2 x 86-1/2-inches.

Quilt Center Assembly Diagram

BORDERS

Note: The yardage given allows for the **BLUE FLORAL** wide outer border strips to be cut on the lengthwise grain (a couple extra inches are allowed for trimming). Cutting the wide border strips lengthwise will eliminate the need for piecing. The yardage given allows for the narrow inner and middle border strips to be cut on the crosswise grain. Diagonally piece the strips together as needed, referring to **Diagonal Piecing** on page 156. Read through **Border** instructions on page 155 for general instructions on adding borders.

Cutting
From **BLUE FLORAL**:
- Cut 9, 2-1/2 x 42-inch inner border strips (cut crossgrain)
- Cut 2, 8-1/2 x 112-inch side outer border strips
  (cut on the lengthwise grain)
- Cut 2, 8-1/2 x 80 top/bottom outer border strips
  (cut on the lengthwise grain)

From **RED PRINT**:
- Cut 9, 1-1/2 x 42-inch middle border strips (cut crossgrain)

Attaching the Borders
Step 1 Attach the 2-1/2-inch wide
   BLUE FLORAL inner border strips.

Step 2 Attach the 1-1/2-inch wide
   RED middle border strips.

Step 3 Attach the 8-1/2-inch wide
   BLUE FLORAL outer border strips.

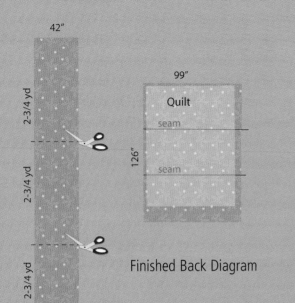

42"

2-3/4 yd

2-3/4 yd

2-3/4 yd

99"

Quilt

seam

126"

seam

Finished Back Diagram

PUTTING IT ALL TOGETHER

Cut the 8-1/4 yard length of backing fabric in thirds crosswise to make 3, 2-3/4 yard lengths. Refer to **Finishing the Quilt** on page 156 for complete instructions

Quilting Suggestions:
- Pieced blocks - **TB73 - 11-1/2" Floral Burst**
- Red lattice segments - channel stitch
- Inner border - channel stitch with diagonal lines
- Outer border - **TB92 - 7" Fence**

THIMBLEBERRIES quilt stencils by Quilting Creations International are available at your local quilt shop or visit www.quiltingcreations.com.

TB 92 7" Fence

TB 73 11-1/2"   Floral Burst

BINDING

Cutting
From **RED PRINT**:
- Cut 11, 2-3/4 x 42-inch strips

Sew the binding to the quilt using a 3/8-inch seam allowance. This measurement will produce a 1/2-inch wide finished double binding. Refer to **Binding** and **Diagonal Piecing** on page 156 for complete instructions.

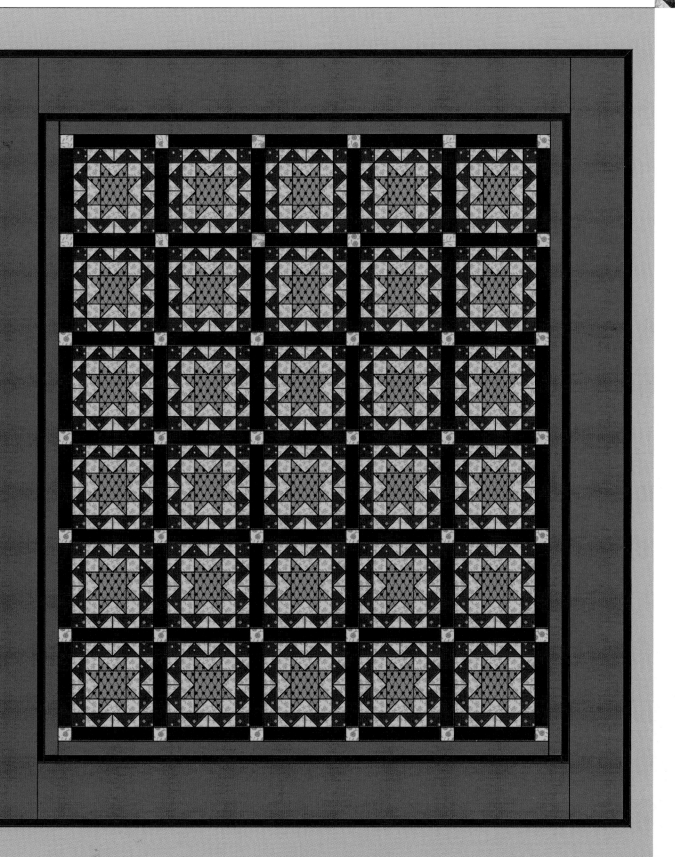

Paint Box Stars Quilt
94 x 108-inches

a season to harvest

In the years since the ancient Celtics celebrated the gathering in of
newly harvested crops and the Pilgrims shared their first Thanksgiving
feast, harvest has been synonymous with a successful planting season.
When a business grows from regional awareness to international
recognition, it is worthy of its harvest. Appropriately enough, an
emerging needlearts business named after a shrub with thimble-shaped
fruit has become known around the world. As a design-driven brand
devoted to the fruit of the needle, Thimbleberries is reaping a harvest
of thousands of Thimbleberries Club members worldwide.

"Autumn has always been my favorite season of the year, with the crisp scent of cool mornings that warm to sunny afternoons—just right for gathering nature's abundant harvest."

When nature's brilliant hues of orange, red and gold first appear, Lynette welcomes the change of seasons because it means bringing in the outdoors with gatherings from her garden. For containers, anything goes—even vintage Halloween treat buckets. Throughout the house, a variety of collected treasures including pottery and chalkware is unified by color—ranging from toasty brown to deep shades of goldenrod—the simplest design principle of all.

During the harvest season, pumpkins of all shapes and sizes abound and take center stage in tabletop displays. In the background, the vintage yardsticks framed as art are premiums offered long ago by local businesses and collected from hardware stores by Lynette's father. It's a sweet remembrance of his frugality.

Harvest Fat Quarter Baskets Quilt

78-inches square

Fabrics and Supplies

16 fat quarters (18 x 20-inch rectangles) of **ASSORTED DARK PRINTS** for baskets
1-1/2 yards **BEIGE PRINT** for basket background
1-1/3 yards **TAN PRINT** for middle border and side/corner triangles
3/8 yard **RED PRINT** for inner border
1-3/4 yards **GREEN PRINT** for outer border
3/4 yard **RED PRINT** for binding
4-2/3 yards for backing
quilt batting, at least 84-inches square

Before beginning this project, read through **Getting Started** on page 154.

BASKET BLOCKS

Makes 64 blocks - Make 4 from each fat quarter
(3 basket blocks will be used for the pieced quilt back)

Cutting - Refer to Cutting Diagram on page 78.

From **each** of the **16 ASSORTED DARK PRINTS**:
• Cut 2, 8-inch squares. Cut the squares in half diagonally to make 4 triangles (a total of 64).

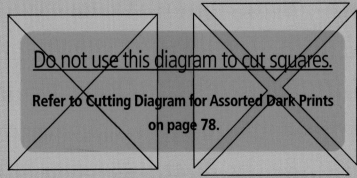

Do not use this diagram to cut squares.

Refer to Cutting Diagram for Assorted Dark Prints on page 78.

- Cut 4, 1-1/2 x 12-inch strips. From the strips cut:
  4, 1-1/2 x 5-1/2-inch rectangles
  4, 1-1/2 x 3-1/2-inch rectangles

- Cut 1, 4-1/2 x 10-1/2-inch rectangle from **13** of the **DARK PRINTS**. Set the 13 rectangles aside to be used for the pieced quilt back.

Cutting Diagram for Assorted Dark Prints

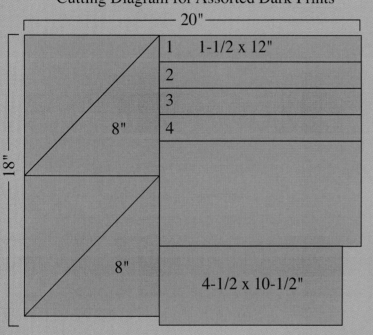

From **BEIGE PRINT**:
- Cut 3, 3-1/2 x 42-inch strips. From the strips cut:
  32, 3-1/2-inch squares
- Cut 13, 1-3/4 x 42-inch strips. From the strips cut:
  64, 1-3/4 x 8-inch rectangles
- Cut 10, 1-3/4 x 42-inch strips. From the strips cut:
  64, 1-3/4 x 5-1/2-inch rectangles

Piecing

Step 1 Sew a pair of 1-1/2 x 3-1/2-inch **DARK PRINT** rectangles to the top/bottom edges of the 3-1/2-inch **BEIGE** square; press. Sew a pair of matching 1-1/2 x 5-1/2-inch **DARK PRINT** rectangles to the side edges of the square; press.

Step 2 Sew the 1-3/4 x 5-1/2-inch **BEIGE** rectangles to the top/bottom edges of the square and the 1-3/4 x 8-inch **BEIGE** rectangles to the side edges. <u>At this point each square should measure 8-inches square.</u>

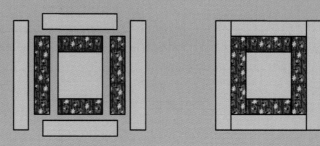

Make 32

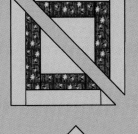

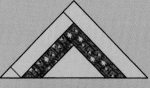

Step 3 Cut each pieced square in half diagonally to make 64 handle units.

Step 4 Sew a matching **DARK PRINT** triangle to each handle unit being careful not to stretch the bias seams; press. <u>At this point each basket block should measure 7-5/8-inches square.</u> Trim if needed.

QUILT CENTER

Note: The side and corner triangles are larger than necessary and will be trimmed before the borders are added.

Make 64

Cutting
From **TAN PRINT**:
- Cut 2, 12-1/2 x 42-inch strips. From the strips cut: 5, 12-1/2-inch squares. Cut the squares diagonally into quarters to make 20 side triangles.

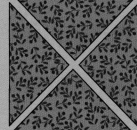

Side Triangles

Also cut 2, 7-1/2-inch squares. Cut the squares in half diagonally to make 4 corner triangles.

Corner
Triangles

Quilt Center Assembly

Step 1 Referring to the quilt center assembly diagram, lay out the basket blocks and side triangles in diagonal rows. Sew together the blocks and side triangles. Press the seam allowances in alternating directions by rows so the seams will fit snugly together with less bulk.

Step 2 Pin the rows together at the block intersections; sew together and press. Sew the corner triangles to the quilt center; press.

Step 3 Trim away the excess fabric from the side/corner triangles taking care to allow a 1/4-inch seam allowance beyond the corners of each block. Refer to **Trimming Side and Corner Triangles** on page 81 for complete instructions.

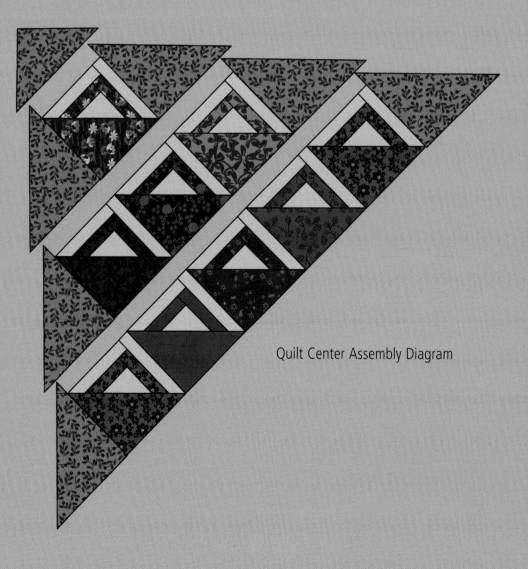

Quilt Center Assembly Diagram

Trimming Side and Corner Triangles

Begin at a corner by lining up your ruler 1/4-inch beyond the points of the corners of the blocks as shown. Cut along the edge of the ruler. Repeat this procedure on all four sides of the quilt top.

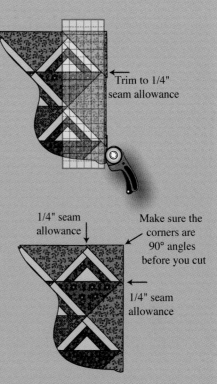

Trim to 1/4"
seam allowance

1/4" seam
allowance

Make sure the
corners are
90° angles
before you cut

1/4" seam
allowance

BORDERS

Note: The yardage given allows for the border strips to be cut on the crosswise grain. Diagonally piece the strips together as needed referring to **Diagonal Piecing** instructions on page 156. Read through **Border** instructions on page 155 for general instructions on adding borders.

Cutting
From **RED PRINT**:
• Cut 7, 1-1/2 x 42-inch inner border strips

From **TAN PRINT**:
• Cut 7, 2-1/2 x 42-inch middle border strips

From **GREEN PRINT**:
• Cut 9, 6-1/2 x 42-inch outer border strips

Attaching the Borders
Step 1 Attach the 1-1/2-inch wide **RED** inner border strips.

Step 2 Attach the 2-1/2-inch wide **TAN** middle border strips.

Step 3 Attach the 6-1/2-inch wide **GREEN** outer border strips.

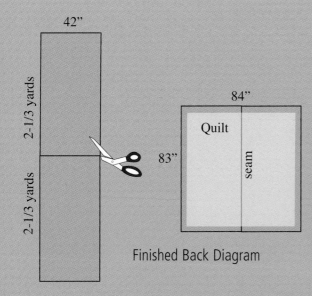

42"

2-1/3 yards

2-1/3 yards

84"

Quilt

seam

83"

Finished Back Diagram

PUTTING IT ALL TOGETHER
Refer to pages 84-85 for the **Harvest Fat Quarter Baskets Pieced Back** instructions. If making a **Plain Back**, continue here.

For **Plain Back**: cut the 4-2/3 yard length of backing fabric in half crosswise to make 2, 2-1/3 yard lengths. Refer to **Finishing the Quilt** on page 156 for complete instructions.

QUILTING SUGGESTIONS:
- **BEIGE** block triangles - echo quilt
- Basket bases - use 1/2 of **TB6 - 5" Leaf Quartet**
- **TAN** side/corner triangles - echo quilt
- **RED** inner border - stitch in-the-ditch
- **TAN** and **GREEN** borders - crosshatch as one border

THIMBLEBERRIES quilt stencils by Quilting Creations International are available at your local quilt shop or visit www.quiltingcreations.com.

BINDING

Cutting
From **RED PRINT**:
- Cut 8, 2-3/4 x 42-inch strips

Sew the binding to the quilt using a 3/8-inch seam allowance. This measurement will produce a 1/2-inch wide finished double binding. Refer to **Binding** and **Diagonal Piecing** on page 156 for complete instructions.

Harvest Fat Quarter Baskets Quilt
78-inches square

HARVEST FAT QUARTER BASKETS PIECED BACK

Leftover basket blocks and piecing makes this quilt reversible.

To Make a Pieced Back You Will Need:
- The 3 extra basket blocks made previously.
- The 13, 4-1/2 x 10-1/2-inch **DARK PRINT** rectangles cut previously.
- The 4-2/3 yards for backing (**BEIGE PRINT**).

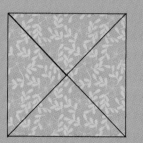
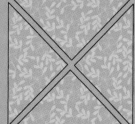

Side Triangles

Cutting
From **BEIGE PRINT**:
- Cut 2, 14-1/2 x 42-inch strips. Sew the short edges together and press to make a 14-1/2 x 82-1/2-inch rectangle.
- Cut 2, 42 x 58-1/2-inch strips. Sew the long edges together and press to make a 58-1/2 x 82-1/2-inch rectangle.
- Cut 1, 12-1/2 x 42-inch strip. From the strip cut: 1, 12-1/2-inch square. Cut the square diagonally into quarters to make 4 side triangles.

Also cut 2, 7-1/2-inch squares. Cut the squares in half diagonally to make 4 corner triangles.

Corner
Triangles

Assembly

Step 1 Lay out the 3 basket blocks and the side triangles in diagonal rows. Sew together the blocks and side triangles. Press the seam allowances toward the side triangles. Pin the rows together at the block intersections; sew together and press. Sew the corner triangles to this unit; press.

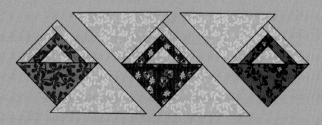
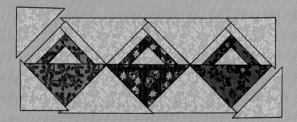

Step 2 Trim away the excess fabric from the side/corner triangles taking care to allow a 1/4-inch seam allowance beyond the corners of each block. Refer to **Trimming Side and Corner Triangles** on page 81 for complete instructions. At this point the basket unit should measure 10-1/2 x 30-1/2-inches.

Step 3 Sew 4 of the 4-1/2 x 10-1/2-inch **DARK PRINT** rectangles together; press. Sew this unit to the left edge of the basket unit; press. Sew 9 of the 4-1/2 x 10-1/2-inch **DARK PRINT** rectangles together; press. Sew this unit to the right edge of the basket unit; press. At this point the basket block unit should measure 10-1/2 x 82-1/2-inches.

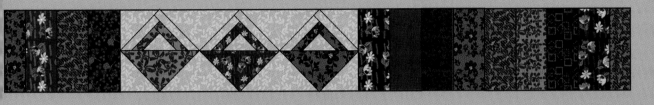

Step 4 Sew the 14-1/2 x 82-1/2-inch **BEIGE** strip to the bottom edge of the basket block unit; press. Sew the 58-1/2 x 82-1/2-inch **BEIGE** strip to the top edge of the unit; press. At this point the pieced back should measure 82-1/2-inches square.

Step 5 Refer to **Finishing the Quilt** on page 156 for complete instructions.

Harvest Fat Quarter Baskets Quilt Pieced Back
78-inches square

Blanket Plaid Quilt

90 x 108-inches

Fabrics and Supplies

4-1/8 yards **RUST PRINT** for blocks, lattice posts, and outer border
2-1/4 yards **BLACK PRINT** for blocks, lattice segments, and middle border
2-1/8 yards **GREEN DIAGONAL PRINT** for blocks and inner border
2-1/4 yards **GOLD PRINT** for lattice segments
1 yard **GREEN DIAGONAL PRINT** for binding
8 yards for backing
quilt batting, at least 95 x 114-inches

Before beginning this project, read through **Getting Started** on page 154.

PIECED BLOCKS

Makes 20 blocks

Cutting
From **RUST PRINT**:
- Cut 8, 4-1/2 x 42-inch strips
- Cut 15, 2-1/2 x 42-inch strips

From **BLACK PRINT**:
- Cut 12, 2-1/2 x 42-inch strips

From **GREEN DIAGONAL PRINT**:
- Cut 10, 4-1/2 x 42-inch strips

Piecing
Step 1 Aligning long edges, sew together 3 of the 2-1/2 x 42-inch **BLACK** strips and 2 of the 4-1/2 x 42-inch **RUST** strips. Press, referring to page 155 for **Hints and Helps for Pressing Strip Sets**. Make 4 strip sets. Cut the strip sets into segments.

Crosscut 60, 2-1/2- inch wide
segments

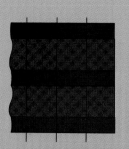

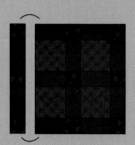

Crosscut 40, 4-1/2-inch
wide segments

Step 2 Aligning long edges, sew together 3 of the 2-1/2 x 42-inch **RUST** strips and 2 of the 4-1/2 x 42-inch **GREEN DIAGONAL PRINT** strips; press. Make 5 strip sets. Cut the strip sets into segments.

Step 3 Referring to the block diagram, sew together 3 of the Step 1 segments and 2 of the Step 2 segments; press. At this point each block should measure 14-1/2-inches square.

Make 20

QUILT CENTER

Cutting
From **GOLD PRINT**:
• Cut 34, 2 x 42-inch strips

From **BLACK PRINT**:
• Cut 17, 1-1/2 x 42-inch strips

From **RUST PRINT**:
• Cut 4, 4-1/2 x 42-inch strips. From the strips cut:
  30, 4-1/2-inch lattice post squares

Quilt Center Assembly
Step 1 Aligning long edges, sew 2 x 42-inch **GOLD** strips to both side edges of a 1-1/2 x 42-inch **BLACK** strip. Press the seam allowances toward the **BLACK** strip, referring to **Hints and Helps for Pressing Strip Sets** on page 155. Make 17 strip sets. (You may need to make more strip sets if your fabric is not 44-inches wide.) Cut the strip sets into segments.

Crosscut 49,14-1/2-inch-long
pieced lattice segments

Step 2 Sew together 4 of the pieced blocks and 5 of the 4-1/2 x 14-1/2-inch pieced lattice segments. Press the seam allowances toward the lattice pieces. At this point each block row should measure 14-1/2 x 76-1/2-inches.

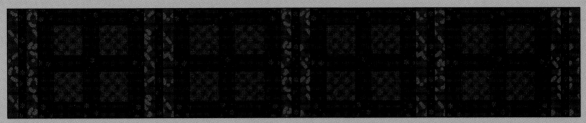

Make 5 block rows

Step 3 Sew together 4 of the 4-1/2 x 14-1/2-inch pieced lattice segments and 5 of the 4-1/2-inch **RUST** lattice post squares. At this point each lattice strip should measure 4-1/2 x 76-1/2-inches.

Make 6 lattice strips

Step 4 Pin the block rows and lattice strips together at the block intersections and sew together. Press the seam allowances toward the lattice strips. At this point the quilt center should measure 76-1/2 x 94-1/2-inches.

BORDERS

Note: The yardage given allows for the border strips to be cut on the crosswise grain. Diagonally piece the strips as needed, referring to page 156 for **Diagonal Piecing** instructions.

Cutting
From **GREEN DIAGONAL PRINT**:
- Cut 10, 2-1/2 x 42-inch inner border strips

From **BLACK PRINT**:
- Cut 10, 1-1/2 x 42-inch middle border strips

From **RUST PRINT**:
- Cut 11, 4-1/2 x 42-inch outer border strips

Attach the Borders

Step 1 Attach the 2-1/2-inch wide **GREEN DIAGONAL PRINT** inner border strips.

Step 2 Attach the 1-1/2-inch wide **BLACK** middle border strips.

Step 3 Attach the 4-1/2-inch wide **RUST** outer border strips.

Finished Back Diagram

PUTTING IT ALL TOGETHER

Cut the 8 yard length of backing fabric in thirds crosswise to make 3, 2-2/3 yard lengths. Refer to **Finishing the Quilt** on page 156 for complete instructions.

Quilting Suggestions:
- Pieced blocks - **TB14 - 11" Bur Oak** (enlarge to 14" square)
- Pieced lattice - **TB28 - 3" Leaf Sketch**
- Lattice post squares - **TB23 - 5" Floral Burst** (use only center flower)
- Three borders quilted as one - **TB44 - 5-1/2" Star Vine Border**

THIMBLEBERRIES quilt stencils by Quilting Creations International are available at your local quilt shop or visit www.quiltingcreations.com.

TB 14 - 11"   Bur Oak

TB 23 - 5"   Floral Burst

TB 44 - 5-1/2"   Star Vine

TB 28 - 3"   Leaf Sketch

BINDING

Cutting
From **GREEN DIAGONAL PRINT**:
• Cut 11, 2-3/4 x 42-inch strips

Sew the binding to the quilt using a 3/8-inch seam allowance. This measurement will produce a 1/2-inch wide finished double binding. Refer to page 156 for **Binding** and **Diagonal Piecing** instructions.

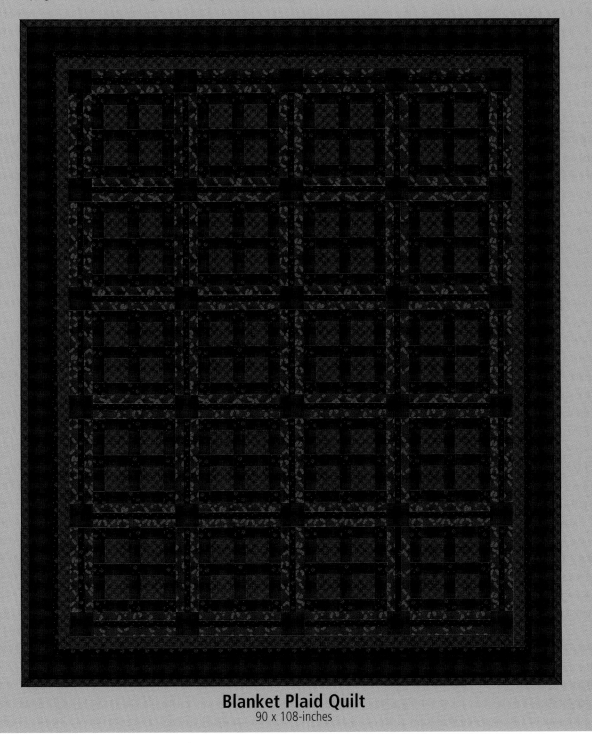

Blanket Plaid Quilt
90 x 108-inches

In downtown Hutchinson, Minnesota the 100-year-old building with original tin ceilings and hardwood floors is solidly planted near the corner of Main Street. It is a refurbished furniture store that was a vital part of the community for more than a century. This old brick and mortar structure has more history and stories to tell than we will ever know.

For many years it has been the home of the Thimbleberries Design Studio. Main Street Cotton Shop, an independent, full-service quilting shop located in the Thimbleberries building, currently stocks the entire line of Thimbleberries fabric, books and patterns as well as many of the new signature products. It has become a destination for Thimbleberries enthusiasts who visit from around the world.

a season to celebrate

Why does the enduring popularity of Thimbleberries continue to grow year after year? Since its inception, the vision for excellence and commitment to quality has not changed, but the brand has expanded far beyond the original audience to reach a marketplace eagerly seeking new adventures in decorating and entertaining. Celebrate with Thimbleberries founder, Lynette Jensen, as she shares a Celebration Sampler Quilt featuring blocks with familiar motifs—from the pine tree to flowers, flying geese, hearts, houses, and stars of all sizes. Best of all, it's designed to welcome you home!

"In looking back to what has brought Thimbleberries to a future bright with promise, I'm reminded that through all the years, we didn't just make quilts. We made history. My contribution is what quilters around the world call Thimbleberries."

Warm up to winter with white. Lynette often celebrates the season by creating a study in serenity and simplicity. Nestled in a bed of greens, clay pots and trays painted white and trimmed with buttons are a heavenly host to candles glowing softly in the evening shadows. With more than enough to go around, store extra buttons in a box to use as a decorative accent.

Dreaming of a white Christmas is as easy as filling the corner cupboard. Stoneware soup toureens surrounded by antique soup bowls serve up an impressive holiday display.

Prairie Pines Wall Quilt

51-inches square

Fabrics and Supplies

1/8 yard each of **10 ASSORTED BEIGE PRINTS** for background
1/2 yard **GREEN PRINT** for trees
1/8 yard **BROWN PRINT** for tree trunks
1/2 yard **BEIGE FLORAL** for side and corner triangles
3/8 yard **RED PRINT** for inner border
3/8 yard **GREEN/RED PRINT** for middle border
1-5/8 yards **GREEN HOLLY PRINT** for outer border
  (cut on the lengthwise grain)
5/8 yard **RED PRINT** for binding
3-1/4 yards for backing
quilt batting, at least 57-inches square
template material (posterboard, manila folder, or template plastic)

Before beginning this project, read through **Getting Started** on page 154.

PRAIRIE PINE BLOCKS
Makes 5 blocks

Make Templates using the shapes on page 106:

Make a copy of the tree patterns on page 106. Glue the copy to your template material. Cut off the marking lines. If you cut beyond to the outside edge of the marking line, you will be adding extra size to the template when you trace onto fabric. Be as accurate as you can when cutting templates. It is critical for precise piecing.

Note: We use a rotary cutter and our old blades to cut straight-edge templates. Mark the blade so you will know right away that it is to be used only for this purpose.

MAKING TEMPLATES

Our patterns include seam allowances. The cutting line is the solid outer line and the stitching line is a dashed line. We have included dots at the seam intersections to help in matching up and pinning the pieces together for accurate placement. Make holes in your templates at the dots with a heavy needle or 1/8-inch paper punch. The holes need to be large enough for the point of a pencil or marker.

Draw around the template (printed side up) on the wrong side of the fabric; this line is the cutting line. When a template is labeled "Reverse," it is to give a left and right version of the same shape. For example, tree trunk Template D is labeled "cut 5 and 5 Reversed." You will need to cut 5 shapes with the template right side up, then turn the template over and cut 5 pieces of Template D Reversed.

With a pencil or marker, mark the seam intersection dots on the fabric pieces. To join two fabric pieces, place them right sides together, and pin them together matching the dots. Sew the two pieces together being careful not to stretch the bias edges. Press the seam allowances to one side, again being careful not to stretch the pieces.

Note: Template plastic can also be used to make templates. Place the plastic on top of a tree pattern and trace it with a fine point permanent marking pen. Transfer all the markings from the pattern onto the template.

Cutting
From **ASSORTED BEIGE PRINTS**:
- Cut 10 of Pattern E
- Cut 10 of Pattern F
- Cut 15 of Pattern G
- Cut 15 of Pattern G Reversed
- Cut 5 of Pattern H
- Cut 5 of Pattern H Reversed

From **GREEN PRINT**:
- Cut 20 of Pattern A
- Cut 10 of Pattern B
- Cut 10 of Pattern C

From **BROWN PRINT**:
- Cut 5 of Pattern D
- Cut 5 of Pattern D Reversed

Piecing

Step 1 For one pine tree block, you will need 4 **GREEN A** pieces, 2 **GREEN B** pieces, 2 **GREEN C** pieces, 1 **BROWN D** piece, 1 **BROWN D** Reversed piece, 2 **BEIGE E** triangles, 2 **BEIGE F** triangles, 3 **BEIGE G** pieces, 3 **BEIGE G** Reversed pieces, 1 **BEIGE H** piece, and 1 **BEIGE H** Reversed piece.

Step 2 Referring to the diagram, pin together a **BEIGE H** piece and a **GREEN A** piece being careful to match the dots. Stitch together. Press the seam allowance toward the **GREEN** fabric. In the same manner pin and sew together:

a **GREEN B** piece to a **BEIGE G** piece
a **GREEN A** piece to a **BEIGE G** piece
a **GREEN C** piece to a **BEIGE G** piece
a **BROWN D** piece to a **BEIGE E** triangle
a **GREEN A** piece to a **BEIGE H** Reversed piece
a **GREEN B** piece to a **BEIGE G** Reversed piece
a **GREEN A** piece to a **BEIGE G** Reversed piece
a **GREEN C** piece to a **BEIGE G** Reversed piece
a **BROWN D** Reversed piece to a **BEIGE E** triangle

Step 3 Referring to the diagram for placement, pin and sew together 5 pieced strips for each half of the tree. Press the seam allowances toward the top of the tree on the left hand side and toward the bottom of the tree on the right hand side. Pin and sew a **BEIGE F** triangle to the bottom of each tree half; press.

Step 4 Pin the tree halves together at the seam lines and sew. Press the center seam allowance open. Square off all blocks so they are the same measurement. <u>The blocks should be approximately 10-inches square.</u>

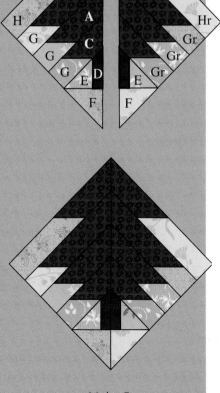

Make 5

QUILT CENTER
Note: The side and corner triangles are larger than necessary and will be trimmed before the borders are added.

Cutting
From **BEIGE FLORAL**:
- Cut 1, 15-1/2 x 42-inch strip. From the strip cut:
  1, 15-1/2-inch square. Cut the square into quarters diagonally to make 4 side triangles.

Also cut 2, 9-inch squares. Cut each square in half diagonally for a total of 4 corner triangles.

Side Triangles

Corner Triangles

Quilt Center Assembly

Quilt Center Assembly

Step 1 Referring to the quilt center assembly diagram for block placement, sew the pieced tree blocks and **BEIGE FLORAL** side triangles together in diagonal rows. Press the seam allowances in alternating directions by rows so the seams will fit snugly together with less bulk.

Step 2 Pin the rows together at the block intersections; sew the rows together and press.

Step 3 Sew the **BEIGE FLORAL** corner triangles to the quilt center; press.

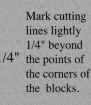

Step 4 Trim away the excess fabric from the side and corner triangles, taking care to allow a 1/4-inch seam allowance beyond the corners of each block. Refer to **Trimming the Side and Corner Triangles** for complete instructions.

Trimming Side and Corner Triangles

- Begin at a corner by lining up your ruler 1/4-inch beyond the points of the block corners as shown. Cut along the edge of the ruler. Repeat this procedure on all four sides of the quilt top.

Mark cutting lines lightly 1/4" beyond the points of the corners of the blocks.

1/4"

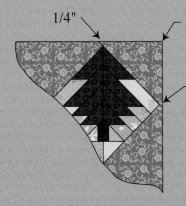

1/4"

Make sure the corners are 90° angles before you cut.

1/4"

BORDERS

Note: The yardage given allows for the **GREEN HOLLY** wide outer border strips to be cut on the lengthwise grain (a couple extra inches are allowed for trimming). Cutting the wide border strips lengthwise will eliminate the need for piecing. The yardage given allows for the narrow inner and middle border strips to be cut on the crosswise grain. Read through **Border** instructions on page 155 for general instructions on adding borders.

Cutting
From **RED PRINT:**
- Cut 4, 2-1/2 x 42-inch inner border strips

From **GREEN/RED PRINT:**
- Cut 4, 2-1/2 x 42-inch middle border strips

From **GREEN HOLLY PRINT:**
- Cut 2, 8-1/2 x 55-inch side outer border strips (cut on the lengthwise grain)
- Cut 2, 8-1/2 x 36-inch top/bottom outer border strips (cut on the lengthwise grain)

Attaching the Borders

Step 1 Attach the 2-1/2-inch wide **RED PRINT** inner border strips.

Step 2 Attach the 2-1/2-inch wide **GREEN/RED PRINT** middle border strips.

Step 3 Attach the 8-1/2-inch wide **GREEN HOLLY PRINT** outer border strips.

PUTTING IT ALL TOGETHER

Cut the 3-1/4 yard length of backing fabric in half crosswise to make 2, 1-5/8 yard lengths. Refer to **Finishing the Quilt** on page 156 for complete instructions.

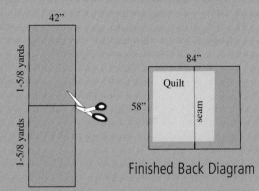

Finished Back Diagram

Quilting Suggestions:
- Trees - stitch in-the-ditch and echo quilt in branches
- Trunks - narrow channel stitches
- **BEIGE** tree backgrounds - stipple
- **BEIGE FLORAL** side/corner triangles - stitch in-the-ditch and echo quilt
- **RED** and **GREEN** borders - quilt as one border with **TB28 - 3" Leaf Sketch**
- **GREEN HOLLY** outer border - meander or channel stitch

THIMBLEBERRIES quilt stencils by Quilting Creations International are available at your local quilt shop or visit www.quiltingcreations.com.

TB 28 - 3"   Leaf Sketch

BINDING

Cutting
From **RED PRINT:**
- Cut 6, 2-3/4 x 42-inch strips

Sew the binding to the quilt using a 3/8-inch seam allowance. This measurement will produce a 1/2-inch wide finished double binding. Refer to page 156 for **Binding** and **Diagonal Piecing** instructions.

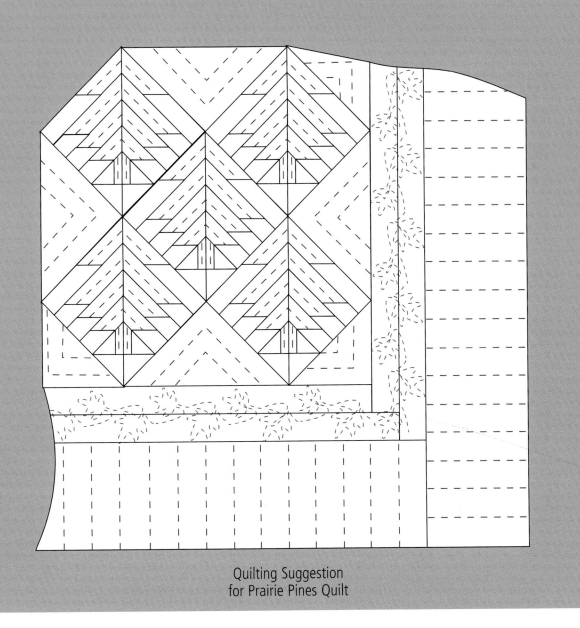

Quilting Suggestion
for Prairie Pines Quilt

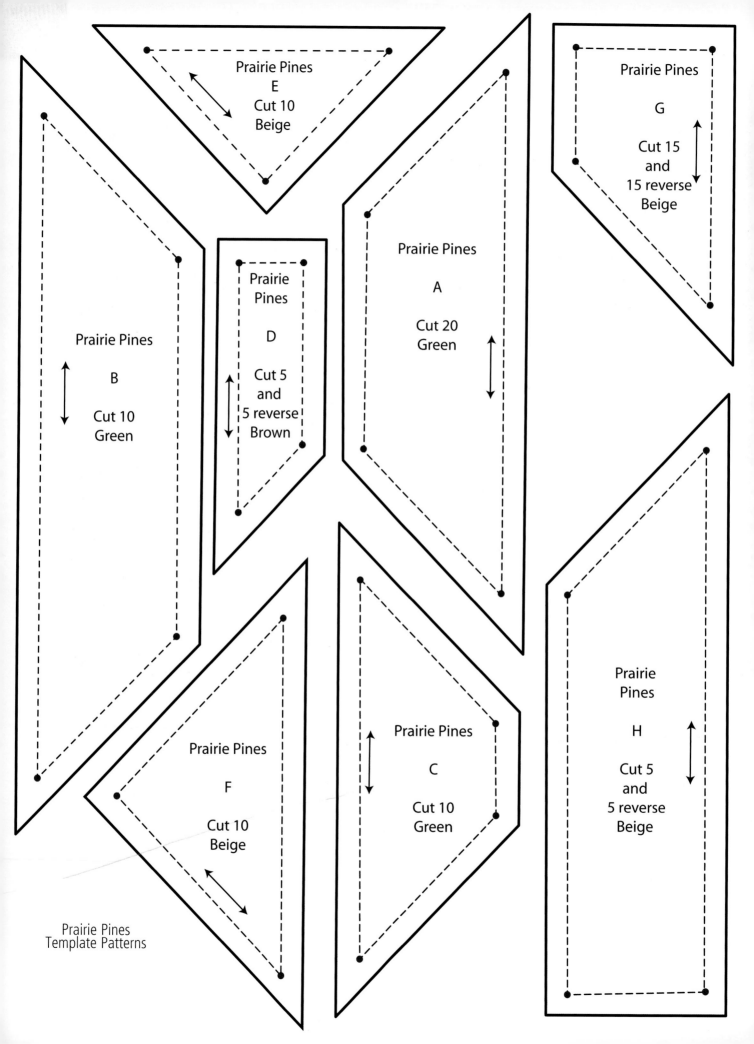

Prairie Pines
E
Cut 10
Beige

Prairie Pines
G
Cut 15
and
15 reverse
Beige

Prairie Pines
B
Cut 10
Green

Prairie
Pines
D
Cut 5
and
5 reverse
Brown

Prairie Pines
A
Cut 20
Green

Prairie Pines
F
Cut 10
Beige

Prairie Pines
C
Cut 10
Green

Prairie
Pines
H
Cut 5
and
5 reverse
Beige

Prairie Pines
Template Patterns

Prairie Pines Quilt
51-inches square

"Prairie Pines is a fine tribute to my journey from avid quilt collector to quiltmaker to designer. As the first pattern I designed, it has stood the test of time since it adapts well to a variety of alternate colorways."

From Thanksgiving to New Year's Day, Lynette takes advantage of Minnesota's long winter season by celebrating every day of the week as a holiday housewarming. From dawn to twilight and throughout the evening, dozens of twinkling lights, candles and lamps scattered throughout her home cast a warm glow on everyday activities. In the living room, firelight reflects all the comforts of home.

Forest View Quilt

64 x 72-inches

Fabrics and Supplies

1-1/4 yards **RED PRINT #1** for hourglass blocks and outer border

1/2 yard **BEIGE PRINT #1** for background

1-1/8 yards **GREEN PRINT** for inner border, dogtooth border, corner squares, and tree blocks

1-1/2 yards **RED PRINT #2** for inner border, star blocks, dogtooth border, and middle border

1-1/8 yards **GREEN FLORAL** for tree blocks and middle border

2 yards **BEIGE PRINT #2** for background, middle border, and dogtooth border

2/3 yard **GREEN PRINT** for binding

4 yards for backing

quilt batting, at least 70 x 78-inches

Before beginning this project, read through **Getting Started** on page 154.

Note: Accuracy is a must for this pattern as you will be adding pieced borders.

HOURGLASS BLOCKS
Makes 15 blocks

Cutting
From **RED PRINT #1**:
- Cut 1, 5-1/4 x 42-inch strip. From the strip cut: 8, 5-1/4-inch squares. Cut the squares diagonally into quarters to make 32 triangles. You will be using only 30 triangles.

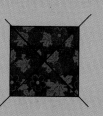 

From **BEIGE PRINT #1**:
- Cut 1, 5-1/4 x 42-inch strip. From the strip cut: 8, 5-1/4-inch squares. Cut the squares diagonally into quarters to make 32 triangles. You will be using only 30 triangles.

Bias edges

Make 30
triangle units

Make 15
hourglass blocks

Piecing

Step 1 With right sides together, layer a **RED #1** triangle on a **BEIGE #1** triangle. Stitch along the bias edge being careful not to stretch the triangles. Press the seam allowance toward the **RED #1** triangle. Repeat for the remaining **RED #1** and **BEIGE #1** triangles. Sew the triangle units together in pairs; press. At this point each hourglass block should measure 4-1/2-inches square.

Step 2 Sew the hourglass blocks together in 5 rows of 3 blocks each. Press the seam allowances in alternating directions by rows so the seams will fit snugly together with less bulk.

Step 3 Pin the rows together at the block intersections; sew the rows together; press. At this point the quilt center should measure 12-1/2 x 20-1/2-inches.

INNER BORDERS and DOGTOOTH BORDER

Note: The yardage given allows for the border strips to be cut on the crosswise grain. Diagonally piece the strips as needed, referring to page 156 for **Diagonal Piecing** instructions. Read through **Border** instructions on page 155 for general instructions on adding borders.

Cutting

From **GREEN PRINT**:
- Cut 3, 2-1/2 x 42-inch first inner border strips
- Cut 3 more 2-1/2 x 42-inch strips. From the strips cut:
  20, 2-1/2 x 4-1/2-inch rectangles
  4, 2-1/2-inch corner squares

From **BEIGE PRINT #1**:
- Cut 3, 2-1/2 x 42-inch strips. From the strips cut:
  40, 2-1/2-inch squares

From **RED PRINT #2**:
- Cut 3, 2-1/2 x 42-inch second inner border strips

Piecing

Step 1 Attach the 2-1/2-inch wide **GREEN** inner border strips.

Step 2 With right sides together, position a 2-1/2-inch **BEIGE #1** square on the corner of a 2-1/2 x 4-1/2-inch **GREEN** rectangle. Draw a diagonal line on the square and stitch on the line. Trim the seam allowance to 1/4-inch. Press the seam allowance toward the dark fabric. Repeat this process at the opposite corner of the rectangle. Press the seam allowance toward the light fabric.

Make 20

Step 3 For the top/bottom dogtooth borders, sew 4 of the Step 2 units together; press. At this point each dogtooth border should measure 2-1/2 x 16-1/2-inches. Sew the borders to the top/bottom edges of the quilt center; press.

Make 2

Step 4 For the side dogtooth borders, sew 6 of the Step 2 units together; press. Sew 2-1/2-inch **GREEN** corner squares to both ends of the border strips; press. At this point each dogtooth border should measure 2-1/2 x 28-1/2-inches. Sew the border strips to the side edges of the quilt center; press.

Make 2

Step 5 Attach the 2-1/2-inch wide **RED #2** second inner border strips.

TREE BLOCKS

Makes 8 **GREEN PRINT** blocks
Makes 6 **GREEN FLORAL** blocks

Cutting

From **GREEN PRINT**:
- Cut 2, 4-1/2 x 42-inch strips. From the strips cut:
  8, 4-1/2 x 8-1/2-inch rectangles
- Cut 4, 2-1/2 x 42-inch strips. From the strips cut:
  16, 2-1/2 x 8-1/2-inch rectangles

From **GREEN FLORAL**:
- Cut 2, 4-1/2 x 42-inch strips. From the strips cut:
  6, 4-1/2 x 8-1/2-inch rectangles
- Cut 3, 2-1/2 x 42-inch strips. From the strips cut:
  12, 2-1/2 x 8-1/2-inch rectangles

From **BEIGE PRINT #2**:
- Cut 4, 4-1/2 x 42-inch strips. From the strips cut:
  28, 4-1/2-inch squares
- Cut 4, 2-1/2 x 42-inch strips. From the strips cut:
  56, 2-1/2-inch squares

Piecing

Step 1 With right sides together, position a 4-1/2-inch **BEIGE #2** square on the corner of a 4-1/2 x 8-1/2-inch **GREEN PRINT** rectangle. Draw a diagonal line on the square: stitch and trim. Press the seam allowance toward the dark fabric. Repeat this process at the opposite corner of the rectangle. Press the seam allowance toward the light fabric. Repeat this step using the 4-1/2 x 8-1/2-inch **GREEN FLORAL** rectangles.

Make 8 using **GREEN PRINT**
Make 6 using **GREEN FLORAL**

Step 2 With right sides together, position 2-1/2-inch **BEIGE #2** squares on the corners of a 2-1/2 x 8-1/2-inch **GREEN PRINT** rectangle. Draw a diagonal line on the squares; stitch, trim, and press. Repeat this process using the 2-1/2 x 8-1/2-inch **GREEN FLORAL** rectangles.

Make 16 using **GREEN PRINT**
Make 12 using **GREEN FLORAL**

Make 8 using **GREEN PRINT**
Make 6 using **GREEN FLORAL**

Step 3 Referring to the block diagram, sew together 1 of the Step 1 **GREEN PRINT** units and 2 of the Step 2 **GREEN PRINT** units; press. <u>At this point each tree block should measure 8-1/2-inches square.</u> Repeat this process using the **GREEN FLORAL** Step 1 and Step 2 units.

Step 4 Sew **GREEN PRINT** tree blocks to both side edges of a **GREEN FLORAL** tree block; press. Make 2 tree units. At this point each tree unit should measure 8-1/2 x 24-1/2-inches. Sew the tree units to the top/bottom edges of the quilt center; press.

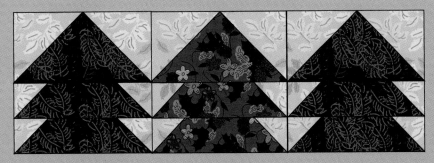

Make 2

Step 5 Sew 2 of the **GREEN FLORAL** tree blocks together and sew a **GREEN PRINT** tree block to both side edges; press. Make 2 tree units. At this point each tree unit should measure 8-1/2 x 32-1/2-inches. The tree units will be sewn to the quilt center after completing the star blocks.

STAR BLOCKS
Makes 4 blocks

Cutting
From **RED PRINT #2**:
- Cut 1, 4-1/2 x 42-inch strip. From the strip cut:
  4, 4-1/2-inch squares
- Cut 2, 2-1/2 x 42-inch strips. From the strips cut:
  32, 2-1/2-inch squares

From **BEIGE PRINT #2**:
- Cut 3, 2-1/2 x 42-inch strips. From the strips cut:
  16, 2-1/2 x 4-1/2-inch rectangles
  16, 2-1/2-inch squares

Piecing
Step 1 Position a 2-1/2-inch **RED #2** square on the corner of a 2-1/2 x 4-1/2-inch **BEIGE #2** rectangle. Draw a diagonal line on the square; stitch, trim, and press. Repeat this process at the opposite corner of the rectangle.

Make 16 star points

Make 4

Step 2 Sew star points to the top/bottom edges of a 4-1/2-inch **RED #2** square; press. Sew 2-1/2-inch **BEIGE #2** squares to both ends of the remaining star point units; press. Sew the units to both side edges of the square; press. <u>At this point each star block should measure 8-1/2-inches square.</u>

Step 3 Sew the star blocks to the ends of both remaining tree units; press. <u>At this point each tree/star unit should measure 8-1/2 x 48-1/2-inches.</u> Sew the units to both side edges of the quilt center; press.

Make 2

BORDERS
Note: The yardage given allows for the border strips to be cut on the crosswise grain. Diagonally piece the strips as needed. Read through **Border** instructions on page 155 for general instructions on adding borders.

Cutting
From **BEIGE PRINT #2**:
- Cut 4, 2-7/8-inch squares
- Cut 5, 2-1/2 x 42-inch first middle border strips
- Cut 6 more 2-1/2 x 42-inch strips. From the strips cut:
  88, 2-1/2-inch squares

From **RED PRINT #2**:
- Cut 4, 2-7/8-inch squares
- Cut 6, 2-1/2 x 42-inch second middle border strips
- Cut 6 more 2-1/2 x 42-inch strips. From the strips cut:
  44, 2-12 x 4-1/2-inch rectangles
  4, 2-1/2-inch squares

From **GREEN FLORAL**:
- Cut 7, 2-1/2 x 42-inch third middle border strips

From **RED PRINT #1**:
- Cut 7, 4-1/2 x 42-inch outer border strips

Assembling and Attaching the Borders

Step 1 Attach the 2-1/2-inch wide **BEIGE #2** first middle border strips.

Step 2 With right sides together, position a 2-1/2-inch **BEIGE #2** square on the corner of a 2-1/2 x 4-1/2-inch **RED #2** rectangle. Draw a diagonal line on the square; stitch and trim. Press the seam allowance toward the dark fabric. Repeat this process at the opposite corner of the rectangle. Press the seam allowance toward the light fabric.

Make 44

Step 3 For the top/bottom dogtooth borders, sew together 10 of the Step 2 units; press. For the side dogtooth borders, sew together 12 of the Step 2 units; press.

Step 4 With right sides together, layer the 2-7/8-inch **BEIGE #2** and **RED #2** squares in pairs. Press together, but do not sew. Cut the layered squares in half diagonally to make 8 sets of triangles. Stitch 1/4-inch from the diagonal edge of each pair of triangles; press. <u>At this point each triangle-pieced square should measure 2-1/2-inches square.</u>

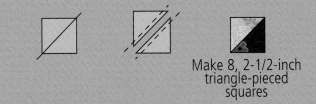

Make 8, 2-1/2-inch
triangle-pieced
squares

Step 5 Referring to the quilt diagram on page 121, sew a Step 4 triangle-pieced square to both ends of the top/bottom dogtooth borders; press. <u>At this point each dogtooth border should measure 2-1/2 x 44-1/2-inches.</u> Sew the borders to the quilt center; press.

Step 6 Sew a Step 4 triangle-pieced square to both ends of the side dogtooth borders. Sew 2-1/2-inch **RED #2** squares to both ends of the side borders; press. <u>At this point each dogtooth border should measure 2-1/2 x 56-1/2-inches.</u> Sew the borders to the quilt center; press.

Step 7 Attach the 2-1/2-inch wide **RED #2** second middle border strips, the 2-1/2-inch wide **GREEN FLORAL** third middle border strips, and the 4-1/2-inch wide **RED #1** outer border strips.

PUTTING IT ALL TOGETHER

Cut the 4 yard length of backing fabric in half crosswise to make 2, 2 yard lengths. Refer to **Finishing the Quilt** on page156 for complete instructions.

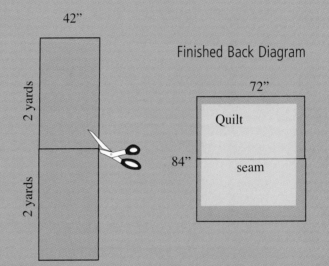
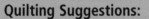

Quilting Suggestions:
- Hourglass blocks - stitch in-the-ditch
- Trees - quilt side to side to look like boughs
- Meander the rest of the quilt omitting the **BEIGE** in the dogtooth border

THIMBLEBERRIES quilt stencils by Quilting Creations International are available at your local quilt shop or visit www.quiltingcreations.com.

BINDING

Cutting
From **GREEN PRINT**:
- Cut 7, 2-3/4 x 42-inch strips

Sew the binding to the quilt using a 3/8-inch seam allowance. This measurement will produce a 1/2-inch wide finished double binding. Refer to page 156 for **Binding** and **Diagonal Piecing** instructions.

Forest View Quilt
64 x 72-inches

Countryside Wreath Wall Quilt

38-inches square

Fabrics and Supplies

1/8 yard each of **12 COORDINATING GREEN PRINTS** for wreath

1/8 yard each of **5 COORDINATING RED PRINTS** for berries and bow

2/3 yard **TAN PRINT** for background and inner border

3/4 yard **BROWN/GREEN/RED BERRY PRINT** for borders and corner squares

3/4 yard **BROWN/GREEN FLORAL** for pieced border

3/8 yard **GREEN DIAGONAL PRINT** for binding

1-1/4 yards for backing

quilt batting, at least 44-inches square

Before beginning this project, read through **Getting Started** on page 154.

QUILT CENTER

Cutting
Note: You can cut extra squares to allow for more combinations of squares and triangles to achieve a scrappier look.

From **12 COORDINATING GREEN PRINTS**:
• Cut at least 17, 2-7/8-inch assorted squares
• Cut at least 25, 2-1/2-inch assorted squares

From **5 COORDINATING RED PRINTS**:
• Cut at least 3, 2-7/8-inch assorted squares
• Cut at least 11, 2-1/2-inch assorted squares

From **TAN PRINT**:
- Cut 1, 6-1/2 x 42-inch strip. From the strip cut:
  5, 6-1/2-inch squares
- Cut 1, 2-7/8 x 42-inch strip. From the strip cut:
  at least 4, 2-7/8-inch squares
- Cut 2, 2-1/2 x 42-inch strips. From the strips cut:
  4, 2-1/2 x 6-1/2-inch rectangles
  12, 2-1/2-inch squares
- Cut 2, 1-1/2 x 24-1/2-inch strips
- Cut 2, 1-1/2 x 22-1/2-inch strips

Piecing the Sections

Step 1 With right sides together, position 2 of the 2-1/2-inch **GREEN** squares on the corners of a 2-1/2 x 6-1/2-inch **TAN** rectangle; press. Draw diagonal lines on the squares and stitch on the lines. Trim the seam allowances to 1/4-inch; press. Sew 2-1/2-inch **TAN** squares to both ends of the unit; press. <u>At this point each unit should measure 2-1/2 x 10-1/2-inches.</u>

Make 3

Step 2 With right sides together, layer 12 of the 2-7/8-inch **GREEN** squares together in 6 pairs. Cut the layered squares in half diagonally to make 12 sets of triangles. Stitch 1/4-inch from the diagonal edge of each pair of triangles; press. Six of the triangle-pieced squares will be used in Step 5 and the remaining 6 triangle-pieced squares will be used in Step 14.

Make 12, 2-1/2-inch
triangle-pieced squares

Step 3 With right sides together, layer 3 of the 2-7/8-inch **TAN** squares and 3 of the **GREEN** squares together in pairs. Cut the layered squares in half diagonally to make 6 sets of triangles. Stitch together and press.

Make 6, 2-1/2-inch
triangle-pieced squares

Step 4 Sew 2-1/2-inch **GREEN** squares to both side edges of a 2-1/2-inch **RED** square; press. Sew Step 3 **TAN/GREEN** triangle-pieced squares to both side edges of the unit; press. At this point each unit should measure 2-1/2 x 10-1/2-inches.

Make 3

Step 5 Sew together 3 of the 2-1/2-inch **GREEN** squares; press. Sew Step 2 **GREEN/GREEN** triangle-pieced squares to to both side edges of the unit; press. At this point each unit should measure 2-1/2 x 10-1/2-inches.

Make 3

Step 6 Referring to the Wreath Section diagram, lay out a Step 1 unit, Step 4 unit, and Step 5 unit. Sew the rows together; press. At this point each wreath section should measure 6-1/2 x 10-1/2-inches.

Make 3 Wreath Sections

Step 7 With right sides together, position 2 of the 2-1/2-inch **RED** squares on the corners of a 2-1/2 x 6-1/2-inch **TAN** rectangle; press. Draw diagonal lines on the squares; stitch, trim, and press. Sew 2-1/2-inch **TAN** squares to both ends of the unit; press. At this point the unit should measure 2-1/2 x 10-1/2-inches.

Make 1

Step 8 With right sides together, layer 2 of the 2-7/8-inch **RED** and **GREEN** squares together. Cut the layered squares in half diagonally to make 4 sets of triangles. Stitch together and press.

 Make 4, 2-1/2-inch triangle-pieced squares

Step 9 With right sides together, layer a 2-7/8-inch **TAN** and **RED** square together. Cut the layered square in half diagonally to make 2 sets of triangles. Stitch together and press.

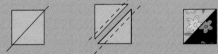 Make 2, 2-1/2-inch triangle-pieced squares

Step 10 Sew Step 8 **RED/GREEN** triangle-pieced squares to both side edges of a 2-1/2-inch **TAN** square; press. Sew 2-1/2-inch **GREEN** squares to both side edges of the unit; press. At this point the unit should measure 2-1/2 x 10-1/2-inches.

 Make 1

Step 11 Sew together 3 of the 2-1/2-inch **RED** squares; press. Sew Step 8 **RED/GREEN** triangle-pieced squares to to both side edges of the unit; press. At this point the unit should measure 2-1/2 x 10-1/2-inches.

 Make 1

Step 12 Sew together 3 of the 2-1/2-inch **RED** squares; press. Sew Step 9 **RED/TAN** triangle-pieced squares to both side edges of the unit; press. At this point the unit should measure 2-1/2 x 10-1/2-inches.

 Make 1

Step 13 Referring to the Bow Section diagram, lay out the Step 7 unit, Step 10 unit, Step 11 unit, and Step 12 unit. Sew the rows together; press. <u>At this point the bow section should measure 8-1/2 x 10-1/2-inches.</u>

Bow Section
Make 1

Step 14 Sew Step 2 **GREEN/GREEN** triangle-pieced squares to both edges of a 2-1/2-inch **TAN** square; press. Make 3 units. Sew 2 of the units to the side edges of the 6-1/2-inch **TAN** square; press. <u>At this point the unit should measure 6-1/2 x 10-1/2-inches.</u>

Make 3

Make 1

Step 15 Sew 2-1/2-inch **GREEN** squares to both side edges of the remaining Step 14 unit; press. <u>At this point the unit should measure 2-1/2 x 10-1/2-inches.</u>

Step 16 Referring to the Center Section diagram, sew the Step 15 unit to the top edge of the Step 14 unit; press. <u>At this point the center section should measure 8-1/2 x 10-1/2-inches.</u>

Center Section
Make 1

Quilt Center Assembly

Step 1 Referring to the quilt center assembly diagram, lay out the wreath, bow, and center sections, and the 6-1/2-inch **TAN** squares. Sew the pieces together in 3 vertical rows; press.

Quilt Center Assembly

Step 2 Sew the rows together; press. <u>At this point the pieced wreath should measure 22-1/2-inches square.</u>

Step 3 Sew the 1-1/2 x 22-1/2-inch **TAN** strips to the top/bottom edges of the quilt center; press.

Step 4 Sew the 1-1/2 x 24-1/2-inch **TAN** strips to the side edges of the quilt center; press.

BORDERS

Note: The yardage given allows for the border strips to be cut on the crosswise grain. Diagonally piece the strips as needed referring to **Diagonal Piecing** on page 156 for complete instructions. Read through **Borders** on page 155 for general instructions on adding borders.

Cutting
From **BROWN/GREEN/RED BERRY PRINT**:
- Cut 4, 2-1/2 x 42-inch inner border strips
- Cut 4, 1-1/2 x 42-inch strips for the pieced border
- Cut 1, 5-1/2 x 42-inch strip. From the strip cut:
  4, 5-1/2-inch corner squares

From **BROWN/GREEN FLORAL**:
- Cut 8, 2-1/2 x 42-inch strips for the pieced border

Attaching the Borders
Step 1 Attach the 2-1/2-inch wide **BROWN/GREEN/RED BERRY PRINT** inner border strips.

Step 2 With long edges aligned, sew 2-1/2-inch wide **BROWN/GREEN FLORAL** strips to the top/bottom edges of a 1-1/2-inch **BROWN/GREEN/ RED BERRY PRINT** strip.

Make 4 pieced borders

Step 3 Measure the quilt from left to right, including the seam allowances, to determine the length of the top/bottom pieced border strips. Cut 2 of the Step 2 pieced borders to this length. Sew the pieced borders to the top/bottom edges of the quilt center; press.

Step 4 Measure the quilt from top to bottom, including the seam allowances but not the borders just added. Cut 2 of the Step 2 pieced borders to this length. Sew the 5-1/2-inch **BROWN/GREEN/RED BERRY PRINT** corner squares to both ends of the pieced border strips; press. Sew the pieced border strips to the side edges of the quilt center; press.

PUTTING IT ALL TOGETHER

Trim the backing and batting so they are 5-inches larger than the quilt top.
Refer to **Finishing the Quilt** on page 156 for complete instructions.

Quilting Suggestions:
- •**BEIGE** 6-inch squares (5 squares) - feathered wreaths and stipple behind wreaths
- •Remaining **BEIGE** areas - stipple
- •Inner Border - stitch in-the-ditch along the inner edge
- •Bow section and **RED** berry squares - stitch in-the-ditch around pieces
- •**GREEN** wreath section - meander
- •Quilt the borders as one border - **TB44 - 5-1/2" Star Vine Border**

THIMBLEBERRIES quilt stencils by Quilting Creations International are available at your local quilt shop or visit www.quiltingcreations.com.

BINDING

Cutting
From **GREEN DIAGONAL PRINT**:
- Cut 4, 2-3/4 x 42-inch strips

Sew the binding to the quilt using a 3/8-inch seam allowance. This measurement will produce a 1/2-inch wide finished double binding. Refer to **Binding** and **Diagonal Piecing** instructions on page 156.

Countryside Wreath Wall Quilt
38-inches square

Countryside Wreath, shown here in an alternate colorway, enjoys a long history of enduring popularity because the pattern adapts easily to existing as well as new Thimbleberries holiday fabric collections.

Thimbleberries Celebration Sampler Quilt

64 x 82-inches

Fabrics and Supplies

5/8 yard **RED PRINT #1** for Block A, Block C, Block H

5/8 yard **RED PRINT #2** for Block E, Block G, Block J, Block K

1/3 yard **GREEN PRINT #1** for Block A, Block E, Block H

3/8 yard **GREEN PRINT #2** for Block E, Block H, Block K

1/3 yard **GREEN PRINT #3** for Block B, Block G

1/4 yard **GOLD PRINT #1** for Block A, Block H, Block L

1/3 yard **GOLD PRINT #2** for Block E, Block J, Block K

1/4 yard **BLUE PRINT #1** for Block A, Block E

1/3 yard **BLUE PRINT #2** for Block D, Block K

1/4 yard **BLUE PRINT #3** for Block I

3/8 yard **BLUE PRINT #4** for Block F, Block J

1/8 yard **BROWN PRINT #1** for Block B

1/4 yard **BROWN PRINT #2** for Block C, Block K

1/8 yard **BLACK PRINT** for Block C, Block G

Assorted Quilt Center Scraps used for spacer rectangles and flying geese border

1-5/8 yards **BEIGE PRINT** for all background and middle border

1 yard **BLACK/BROWN PRINT** for inner and middle borders (cut on crosswise grain)

2-1/2 yards **RUST FLORAL** for outer border (cut on lengthwise grain)

3/4 yard **BLACK/BROWN PRINT** for binding

5 yards backing fabric

quilt batting, at least 70 x 88-inches

paper-backed fusible web for Block G

tear-away fabric stabilizer for Block G

machine embroidery thread of pearl cotton for Block G decorative stitches: black, gold

Before beginning this project, read through Getting Started on page 154.

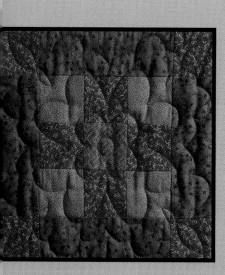

BLOCK A

Cutting

From **RED PRINT #1**:
• Cut 8, 2-1/2-inch squares

From **GREEN PRINT #1**:
• Cut 4, 2-1/2-inch squares

From **GOLD PRINT #1**:
• Cut 1, 2-1/2-inch square

From **BLUE PRINT #1**:
• Cut 4, 2-1/2 x 6-1/2-inch rectangles

Piecing

Step 1 Sew 2-1/2-inch **GREEN #1** squares to both side edges of 2 of the 2-1/2-inch **RED #1** squares; press. Make 2 units. Sew 2-1/2-inch **RED #1** squares to the side edges of the 2-1/2-inch **GOLD #1** square; press. Sew the 3 units together to make a 9-patch square. <u>At this point the 9-patch square should measure 6-1/2-inches square.</u>

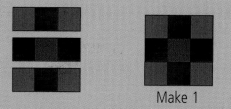

Make 1

Step 2 Sew 2-1/2 x 6-1/2-inch **BLUE #1** rectangles to the top/bottom edges of the 9-patch square; press. Sew 2-1/2-inch **RED #1** squares to both ends of the remaining 2-1/2 x 6-1/2-inch **BLUE #1** rectangles; press. Sew the units to the side edges of the 9-patch square; press. <u>At this point Block A should measure 10-1/2-inches square.</u>

Make 1

BLOCK B
Makes 2 blocks

Cutting
From **GREEN PRINT #3**:
- Cut 2, 3-1/2 x 6-1/2-inch rectangles
- Cut 2, 2-1/2 x 6-1/2-inch rectangles

From **BEIGE PRINT**:
- Cut 4, 3-1/2-inch squares
- Cut 4, 2-1/2-inch squares
- Cut 2, 2-3/4 x 4-inch rectangles

From **BROWN PRINT #1**:
- Cut 1, 2 x 4-inch rectangle

Piecing
Step 1 With right sides together, position a 3-1/2-inch **BEIGE** square on the corner of a 3-1/2 x 6-1/2-inch **GREEN #3** rectangle. Draw a diagonal line on the square; stitch on the line. Trim the seam allowance to 1/4-inch; press. Repeat this process at the opposite corner of the rectangle.

 Make 2

Step 2 With right sides together, position 2-1/2-inch **BEIGE** squares on the corners of a 2-1/2 x 6-1/2-inch **GREEN #3** rectangle. Draw a diagonal line on the squares; stitch, trim, and press.

 Make 2

Step 3 To make the trunk units, sew 2-3/4 x 4-inch **BEIGE** rectangles to both side edges of the 2 x 4-inch **BROWN #1** rectangle; press. Cut the strip set into segments.

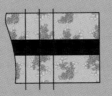 Crosscut 2, 1-1/2-inch wide segments

Step 4 Sew the Step 1, 2, and 3 tree sections together to make the block; press. At this point each Block B should measure 6-1/2-inches square.

Make 2

135

BLOCK C
Makes 2 blocks

Cutting
From BROWN PRINT #2:
- Cut 2, 3-1/2 x 6-1/2-inch rectangles

From BEIGE PRINT:
- Cut 4, 3-1/2-inch squares

From RED PRINT #1:
- Cut 2, 2-1/2 x 3-1/2-inch rectangles
- Cut 2, 1-1/2 x 8-inch strips
- Cut 4, 1-1/2 x 3-1/2-inch rectangles

From BLACK PRINT:
- Cut 1, 1-1/2 x 8-inch strip

Piecing
Step 1 To make the roof units, with right sides together, position a 3-1/2-inch **BEIGE** square on the corner of a 3-1/2 x 6-1/2-inch **BROWN #2** rectangle. Draw a diagonal line on the square; stitch, trim, and press. Repeat this process at the opposite corner of the rectangle.

   Make 2

Step 2 To make the window units, sew the 1-1/2 x 8-inch **RED #1** strips to both side edges of the 1-1/2 x 8-inch **BLACK** strip; press. Cut the strip set into segments.

   Crosscut 4, 1-1/2-inch wide window segments

Step 3 To make the house base units, sew a window segment to both side edges of a 2-1/2 x 3-1/2-inch **RED #1** rectangle; press. Sew 1-1/2 x 3-1/2-inch **RED #1** rectangles to both side edges; press. At this point each house base should measure 3-1/2 x 6-1/2-inches.

Make 2

Step 4 Sew the roof to the top edge of the house base; press. At this point each Block C should measure 6-1/2-inches square.

Make 2

BLOCK D

Cutting

From BEIGE PRINT:
- Cut 1, 2-1/2 x 44-inch strip. From the strip cut: 1, 2-1/2-inch square. The remaining portion of the strip will be used in Step 1.

From BLUE PRINT #2:
- Cut 1, 2-1/2 x 44-inch strip

Piecing

Step 1 With right sides together and aligning long raw edges, sew the 2-1/2 x 44-inch **BEIGE** and **BLUE #2** strips together; press. Cut the strip set into segments.

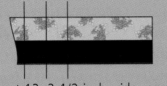

Crosscut 12, 2-1/2-inch wide segments

Step 2 Referring to the diagram, sew the segments together in 3 rows alternating colors. Sew a 2-1/2-inch **BEIGE** square to the third row; press. Sew the rows together; press. <u>At this point Block D should measure 10-1/2-inches square.</u>

Make 1

BLOCK E

Cutting for the Flower Unit

From GOLD PRINT #2:
- Cut 1, 4-1/2-inch square

From BLUE PRINT #1:
- Cut 4, 2-1/2-inch squares

From RED PRINT #2:
- Cut 8, 2-1/2-inch squares

From GREEN PRINT #2:
- Cut 4, 2-1/2 x 4-1/2-inch rectangles
- Cut 4, 2-1/2-inch squares

Piecing the Flower Unit

Step 1 With right sides together, position a 2-1/2-inch **BLUE #1** square on the corner of the 4-1/2-inch **GOLD #2** square. Draw a diagonal line on the **BLUE** square; stitch, trim, and press. Repeat this process at the 3 remaining corners of the **GOLD** square to make the flower center.

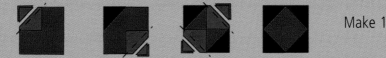 Make 1

Step 2 With right sides together, position a 2-1/2-inch **RED #2** square on the corner of a 2-1/2 x 4-1/2-inch **GREEN #2** rectangle. Draw a diagonal line on the square; stitch, trim, and press. Repeat this process at the opposite corner of the rectangle to make a petal unit.

 Make 4

Step 3 Sew petal units to the top/bottom edges of the flower center; press. Sew 2-1/2-inch **GREEN #2** squares to both ends of the remaining petal units; press. Sew the units to the side edges of the flower center; press. <u>At this point the flower unit should measure 8-1/2-inches square.</u>

Make 1

Cutting for Leaves

From **GREEN PRINT #1**:
• Cut 8, 2-1/2 x 4-1/2-inch rectangles

From **BEIGE PRINT**:
• Cut 12, 2-1/2-inch squares

Piecing the Leaves

Step 1 With right sides together, position a 2-1/2-inch **BEIGE** square on the right corner of a 2-1/2 x 4-1/2-inch **GREEN #2** rectangle. Draw a diagonal line on the square; stitch, trim, and press.

 Make 4

Step 2 Position a 2-1/2-inch **BEIGE** square on the left corner of the remaining **GREEN #2** rectangles. Draw a diagonal line on the square; stitch, trim, and press.

 Make 4

Step 3 Sew the Step 1 and Step 2 units together in pairs. Make 4 leaf units. Sew leaf units to the top/bottom edges of the flower unit; press. Sew 2-1/2-inch **BEIGE** squares to both ends of the remaining leaf units; press. Sew the leaf units to the side edges of the flower unit; press. At this point Block E should measure 12-1/2-inches square.

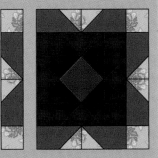

Make 4

Make 1

BLOCK F
Makes 2 blocks

Cutting
From **BLUE PRINT #4**:
• Cut 4, 3-7/8-inch squares

From **BEIGE PRINT**:
• Cut 4, 3-7/8-inch squares

Piecing
Step 1 With right sides together, layer the 3-7/8-inch **BEIGE** and **BLUE #4** squares in pairs. Press together, but do not sew. Cut each layered square in half diagonally to make 8 sets of triangles. Stitch 1/4-inch from the diagonal edge of each pair of triangles; press.

Make 8, 3-1/2-inch
triangle-pieced squares

Step 2 Sew the triangle-pieced squares together in pairs; press. Sew the pairs together to make the pinwheel blocks. At this point each Block F should measure 6-1/2-inches square.

Make 4

Make 2

BLOCK G

Cutting for Leaf Unit
From **GREEN PRINT #3**:
- Cut 4, 1-1/2 x 2-1/2-inch rectangles

From **BEIGE PRINT**:
- Cut 8, 1-1/2-inch squares
- Cut 2, 1-1/2 x 2-1/2-inch rectangles

Piecing the Leaves
Step 1 With right sides together, position a 1-1/2-inch **BEIGE** square on the corner of a 1-1/2 x 2-1/2-inch **GREEN #3** rectangle. Draw a diagonal line on the square; stitch, trim, and press. Repeat this process at the opposite corner of the rectangle. Make 2 units and sew them together. Press the seam allowances up.

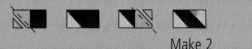   Make 1 left leaf unit

Make 2

Step 2 To make the right leaf unit, repeat Step 1 reversing the direction of the stitching lines. Make 2 units and sew them together. Press the seam allowances down.

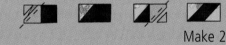   Make 1 right leaf unit

Make 2

Step 3 Sew the right and left leaf units together; press. Sew 1-1/2 x 2-1/2-inch **BEIGE** rectangles to both side edges of the leaf unit; press. <u>At this point the leaf unit should measure 2-1/2 x 6-1/2-inches.</u>

 Make 1

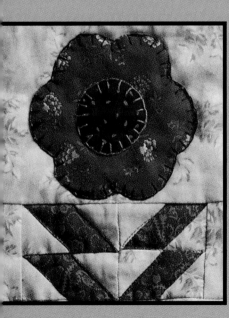

Cutting for Flower Block
From **BEIGE PRINT**:
- Cut 1, 4-1/2 x 6-1/2-inch foundation appliqué rectangle

From **RED PRINT #2**:
- Cut 1, 4-inch square for flower appliqué

From **BLACK PRINT**:
- Cut 1, 2-inch square for flower center appliqué

From fusible web:
- Cut 1, 4-inch square for flower
- Cut 1, 2-inch square for flower center

Assembling the Flower Block

Step 1 Sew the 4-1/2 x 6-1/2-inch **BEIGE** appliqué foundation rectangle to the top edge of the leaf unit; press.

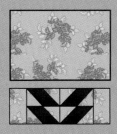

Step 2 Make templates using the flower and flower center shapes on page 142. Trace the template shapes onto the paper side of the fusible web.

Step 3 Following the manufacturer's instructions, fuse the shapes to the wrong side of the 4-inch **RED #2** square and the 2-inch **BLACK** square. Let the fabric cool and cut along the traced line. Peel away the paper backing from the fusible web.

Note: When fusing a large shape like the flower, fuse just the outer edges of the shape so it will not look stiff when finished. To do this, draw a line about 3/8-inch inside the flower and cut away the fusible web on this line.

Step 4 Position the flower and flower center shapes on the **BEIGE** appliqué foundation rectangle so the bottom petals are just above the leaf unit. Fuse in place following the manufacturer's directions.

Make 1

Step 5 We suggest pinning a square of tear-away stabilizer to the backside of the **BEIGE** rectangle so it will lay flat when the machine appliqué is complete. Machine blanket stitch around the shapes using black machine embroidery thread. If you like, you could hand blanket stitch the shapes with pearl cotton. <u>At this point Block G should measure 6-1/2-inches square.</u>

Blanket Stitch

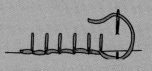

Template for Block G
Flower
Trace 1 onto
fusible web

Template for
Block G
Flower Center
Trace 1 onto
fusible web

BLOCK H

Cutting for Heart Blossom Square
From **RED PRINT #1**:
- Cut 1, 3-1/2-inch square
- Cut 2, 2-1/2 x 3-1/2-inch rectangles

From **GOLD PRINT #1**:
- Cut 1, 2-1/2-inch square

From **BEIGE PRINT**:
- Cut 4, 1-1/4-inch squares

Heart Blossom Assembly
Step 1 With right sides together, position 1-1/4-inch **BEIGE** squares on both upper corners of the 2-1/2 x 3-1/2-inch **RED #1** rectangles. Draw diagonal lines on the squares; stitch, trim, and press.

 Make 2

Step 2 Sew the 2-1/2-inch **GOLD #1** square to the left edge of 1 of the Step 1 units. Press the seam allowance toward the **GOLD** square. Sew the 3-1/2-inch **RED #1** square to the remaining Step 1 unit. Press the seam allowance toward the **RED** square. Sew the units together to make the heart blossom unit; press. <u>At this point the heart blossom unit should measure 5-1/2-inches square.</u>

Make 1

Make 1

 Make 1

Cutting for Leaf Units

From each of **GREEN #1** and **GREEN #2**:
- Cut 2, 2-inch squares
- Cut 2, 2 x 5-1/2-inch rectangles

From **BEIGE PRINT**:
- Cut 4, 2-inch squares
- Cut 1, 1-1/2 x 44-inch border strip

Piecing

Step 1 With right sides together, sew together the 2-inch **GREEN #1** and **GREEN #2** squares; press. <u>At this point the 4-patch unit should measure 3-1/2-inches square.</u>

Make 1

Step 2 To make the right leaf unit, with right sides together, position a 2-inch **BEIGE** square on the right corner of a 2 x 5-1/2-inch **GREEN #1** rectangle. Draw a diagonal line on the square; stitch, trim, and press. Repeat this step using a 2-inch **BEIGE** square and a 2 x 5-1/2-inch **GREEN #2** rectangle. Sew the 2 units together; press. <u>At this point the right leaf unit should measure 3-1/2 x 5-1/2-inches.</u>

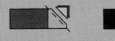

Make 1 right leaf unit

Step 3 To make the left leaf unit, with right sides together, position a 2-inch **BEIGE** square on the left corner of a 2 x 5-1/2-inch **GREEN #1** rectangle. Draw a diagonal line on the square; stitch, trim, and press. Repeat this step using a 2-inch **BEIGE** square and a 2 x 5-1/2-inch **GREEN #2** rectangle. Sew the 2 units together; press. <u>At this point the left leaf unit should measure 3-1/2 x 5-1/2-inches.</u>

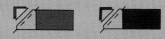

Make 1 left leaf unit

Step 4 Sew the left leaf unit to to the bottom edge of the heart unit. Press the seam allowances toward the heart unit. Sew the right leaf unit to the top edge of the 4-patch unit. Press the seam allowances toward the 4-patch unit. Sew the 2 units together; press. <u>At this point the heart blossom block should measure 8-1/2-inches square.</u>

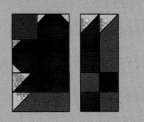

Make 1

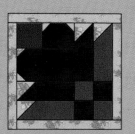

Make 1

Attach the Block Border

Note: The 1-1/2-inch wide **BEIGE** border strips will be attached to the heart blossom block in a log cabin fashion. Do not cut the strip into sections before sewing them to the block.

Refer to the block diagram for border placement. Sew the border strips to the block in a clockwise fashion. After each strip is sewn on, press the strip toward the block and trim the border strip even with the edges of the block. At this point Block H should measure 10-1/2-inches square.

BLOCK I

Cutting
From **BEIGE PRINT**:
• Cut 1, 3-7/8 x 44-inch strip

From **BLUE PRINT #3**:
• Cut 1, 3-7/8 x 44-inch strip

Piecing
Step 1 With right sides together, layer the 3-7/8 x 44-inch **BEIGE** and **BLUE #3** strips. Press together, but do not stitch. Cut the layered strip into squares. Cut each layered square in half diagonally to make 16 sets of triangles. Stitch 1/4-inch from the diagonal edge of each pair of triangles; press.

Crosscut 8, 3-7/8-inch squares

Make 16, 3-1/2-inch triangle-pieced squares

Step 2 Sew the triangle-pieced squares together in 4 rows with 4 squares in each row. Press the seam allowances in alternating directions by rows. Sew the rows together; press. At this point Block I should measure 12-1/2-inches square.

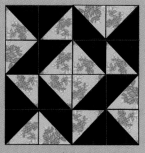

Make 1

BLOCK J

Cutting

From **GOLD PRINT #2**:
- Cut 1, 4-1/2-inch square
- Cut 8, 2-1/2-inch squares

From **BLUE PRINT #4**:
- Cut 4, 4-1/2-inch squares
- Cut 8, 2-1/2-inch squares

From **BEIGE PRINT**:
- Cut 3, 2-1/2 x 22-inch strips
- Cut 4, 2-1/2 x 4-1/2-inch rectangles

From **RED PRINT #2**:
- Cut 3, 2-1/2 x 22-inch strips

Piecing

Step 1 With right sides together and long edges aligned, sew 2-1/2 x 22-inch **RED #2** strips to the top/bottom edges of 1 of the 2-1/2 x 22-inch **BEIGE** strips. Press the strip set referring to **Hints and Helps for Pressing Strip Sets** on page 155. Cut the strip set into segments.

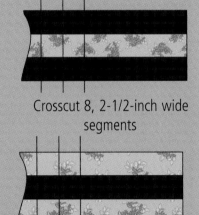

Crosscut 8, 2-1/2-inch wide segments

Crosscut 4, 2-1/2-inch wide segments

Step 2 With right sides together and long edges aligned, sew 2-1/2 x 22-inch **BEIGE** strips to the top/bottom edges of 1 of the 2-1/2 x 22-inch **RED #2** strips; press. Cut the strip set into segments.

Step 3 Sew Step 1 segments to the top/bottom edges of a Step 2 segment; press. At this point each 9-patch unit should measure 6-1/2-inches square.

Make 4

Step 4 With right sides together, position a 2-1/2-inch **GOLD #2** square on the lower corner of a 4-1/2-inch **BLUE #4** square. Draw a diagonal line on the **GOLD** square; stitch, trim, and press. Repeat this process at the adjacent corner of the **BLUE** square.

Make 4

Step 5 With right sides together, position a 2-1/2-inch **BLUE #4** square on the corner of a 2-1/2 x 4-1/2-inch **BEIGE** rectangle. Draw a diagonal line on the square; stitch, trim, and press. Repeat this process at the opposite corner of the rectangle.

 Make 4

Step 6 Sew the Step 5 units to the top edge of the Step 4 units; press. At this point each unit should measure 4-1/2 x 6-1/2-inches.

 Make 4

Step 7 Sew Step 3, 9-patch blocks to the top/bottom edges of 2 of the Step 6 units; press. At this point each unit should measure 6-1/2 x 16-1/2-inches.

Make 2

Step 8 Sew Step 6 units to the top/bottom edges of the 4-1/2-inch **GOLD #2** square; press. At this point the unit should measure 4-1/2 x 16-1/2-inches.

Make 1

Step 9 Sew the 3 units together; press. At this point Block J should measure 16-1/2-inches square.

Make 1

BLOCK K

Cutting

From **RED PRINT #2**, **GREEN PRINT #2**, **GOLD PRINT #2**, **BLUE PRINT #2**:
- Cut 1, 3-3/8-inch square from each fabric
- Cut 1, 3 x 4-1/2-inch rectangle from each fabric

From **BROWN PRINT #2**:
- Cut 1, 4-1/2-inch square

From **BEIGE PRINT**:
- Cut 4, 3-3/8-inch squares
- Cut 4, 3-inch squares

Piecing

Step 1 With right sides together, layer a 3-3/8-inch **BEIGE** square and the 3-3/8-inch **RED** square. Press together, but do not sew. Cut the layered square in half diagonally to make 2 sets of triangles. (You will be using only 1 of the triangle sets.) Stitch 1/4-inch from the diagonal edge of the triangle set; press.

 Make 1, 3-inch triangle-pieced square

Step 2 Repeat Step 1 using the remaining 3-3/8-inch **BEIGE** squares and the 3-3/8-inch **GREEN**, **GOLD**, and **BLUE** squares.

Make 1   Make 1   Make 1

Step 3 With right sides together, position a 3-inch **BEIGE** square on the left corner of the 3 x 4-1/2-inch **RED** rectangle. Draw a diagonal line on the square; stitch, trim, and press.

 Make 1

Step 4 Repeat Step 3 using the remaining 3-inch **BEIGE** squares and the 3 x 4-1/2-inch **GREEN**, **GOLD**, and **BLUE** rectangles.

Make 1   Make 1   Make 1

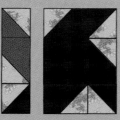

Make 1

Step 5 Referring to the block diagram, sew the Step 3 - 4 units to the top/bottom edges of the 4-1/2-inch **BROWN** square; press. Sew the corresponding Step 1 – 2 triangle-pieced squares to the remaining Step 3 – 4 units; press. Sew the units to the side edges of the center square unit; press. <u>At this point Block K should measure 9-1/2-inches square.</u>

BLOCK L
Makes 3 blocks

Cutting
From **GOLD PRINT #1**:
• Cut 24, 1-1/2-inch squares
• Cut 3, 2-1/2-inch squares

From **BEIGE PRINT**:
• Cut 12, 1-1/2 x 2-1/2-inch rectangles
• Cut 12, 1-1/2-inch squares

Piecing
Step 1 With right sides together, position a 1-1/2-inch **GOLD #1** square on the corner of a 1-1/2 x 2-1/2-inch **BEIGE** rectangle. Draw a diagonal line on the square; stitch, trim, and press. Repeat this process at the opposite corner of the rectangle.

Make 12
star point units

Make 3

Step 2 Sew 2 star point units to the top/bottom edges of the 2-1/2-inch **GOLD** squares; press.

Make 3

Step 3 Sew 1-1/2-inch **BEIGE** squares to both ends of the remaining star point units; press. Sew the units to the side edges of the Step 2 units to complete the stars. <u>At this point each Block L should measure 4-1/2-inches square.</u>

QUILT CENTER

Cutting the Spacer Rectangles

From **ASSORTED SCRAPS** (use remaining quilt center fabrics):

- Cut 1, 4-1/2 x 16-1/2-inch rectangle
- Cut 3, 4-1/2 x 12-1/2-inch rectangles
- Cut 1, 4-1/2 x 6-1/2-inch rectangle
- Cut 1, 3-1/2 x 12-1/2-inch rectangle
- Cut 1, 3-1/2 x 9-1/2-inch rectangle
- Cut 2, 2-1/2 x 12-1/2-inch rectangles
- Cut 1, 2-1/2 x 10-1/2-inch rectangle
- Cut 1, 2-1/2 x 6-1/2-inch rectangle

Quilt Center Assembly

Step 1 The quilt is assembled in 4 horizontal rows. Referring to the quilt center assembly diagram for placement, lay out the prepared blocks and the spacer rectangles. Refer to the assembly diagram for cut sizes of the spacer rectangles.

Step 2 Sew together the blocks and spacer rectangles in rows; press. At this point each row should be 32-1/2-inches long.

Step 3 Sew the rows together; press. At this point the quilt center should measure 32-1/2 x 50-1/2-inches.

Quilt Center Assembly Diagram

BORDERS

Note: The yardage given allows for the wide outer border strips to be cut on the lengthwise grain (a couple extra inches are allowed for trimming). Cutting the wide border strips lengthwise will eliminate the need for piecing. The yardage given allows for the narrow border strips to be cut on the crosswise grain. Diagonally piece the strips as needed, referring to page 156 for **Diagonal Piecing** instructions. Read through **Borders** on page 155 for complete instructions.

Cutting
From **BLACK/BROWN PRINT**:
• Cut 5, 2-1/2 x 44-inch inner border strips
• Cut 7, 2-1/2 x 44-inch middle border strips

From **BEIGE PRINT**:
• Cut 3, 4-1/2 x 44-inch strips for wide middle border
• Cut 5, 2-1/2 x 44-inch strips. From the strips cut:
  80, 2-1/2-inch squares for flying geese

From **ASSORTED SCRAPS** (use remaining quilt center fabrics):
• Cut a total of 40, 2-1/2 x 4-1/2-inch rectangles for flying geese

From **RUST FLORAL** (cut on the lengthwise grain):
• Cut 2, 8-1/2 x 90-inch side outer border strips
• Cut 2, 8-1/2 x 50-inch top/bottom outer border strips

Assembling and Attaching the Borders
Step 1 Attach the 2-1/2-inch wide **BLACK/BROWN** inner border strips.

Step 2 With right sides together, position a 2-1/2-inch **BEIGE** square on the corner of a 2-1/2 x 4-1/2-inch **SCRAP** rectangle. Draw a diagonal line on the square; stitch, trim, and press. Repeat this process at the opposite corner of the rectangle.

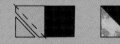

Make 40 flying geese

Step 3 For the top/bottom flying geese borders, randomly sew together 4 flying geese; press. Make 4 flying geese units. <u>At this point each flying geese unit should measure 4-1/2 x 8-1/2-inches.</u>

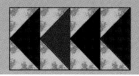

Make 4

Step 4 For the top/bottom borders, measure the quilt center from left to right through the middle, including the seam allowances. Subtract 16-inches from this measurement to allow for 2 flying geese units. Cut 2, 4-1/2-inch wide **BEIGE** strips to this measurement. Sew a flying geese unit to both ends of each **BEIGE** strip; press. At this point each pieced border should measure 4-1/2 x 34-1/2-inches. Sew the pieced border strips to the top/bottom edges of the quilt center; press.

Make 2

Step 5 Referring to the diagram for placement, randomly sew together 6 flying geese for the side borders; press. At this point each flying geese unit should measure 4-1/2 x 12-1/2-inches.

Make 2 flying geese units

Make 2 flying geese units

Step 6 For the side borders, measure the quilt center from top to bottom through the middle, including the seam allowances. Subtract 24-inches from this measurement to allow for 2 flying geese units. Cut 2, 4-1/2-inch wide **BEIGE** strips to this measurement for the side borders. Sew a flying geese unit to both ends of each **BEIGE** strip; press. At this point each pieced border should measure 4-1/2 x 62-1/2-inches. Sew the pieced border strips to the side edges of the quilt center; press.

Step 7 Attach the 2-1/2-inch wide **BLACK/BROWN** middle border strips.

Step 8 Attach the 8-1/2-inch wide **RUST FLORAL** outer border strips.

PUTTING IT ALL TOGETHER

Cut the 5 yard length of backing fabric in half crosswise to make 2, 2-1/2-yard lengths. Refer to **Finishing the Quilt** on page 156 for complete instructions.

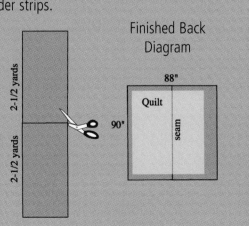

Finished Back Diagram

Quilting Suggestions:

- Block A - **TB24 - 9" Floral Burst**
- Block B tree - loops to make boughs
- Block C house - echo in roof, in-the-ditch on house
- Block D checkerboard - big X in each square
- Block E Cottage Flower - **TB73 - 11-1/2" Floral Burst**
- Block F pinwheel - stipple in **BEIGE**
- Block G flower - in-the-ditch around shapes
- Block H Heart Blossom - **TB6 - 5" Leaf Quartet** and in-the-ditch around leaves
- Block I - echo in color, stipple in **BEIGE**
- Block J - point-to-point in star, echo in **BLUE**, X in 9-patch
- Block K paddlewheel - echo in paddles, X in center
- Block L stars - point-to-point
- Spacer rectangles - channel, Xs, **TB30 - 1-1/2" Beadwork**, **TB78 - 3-1/2" x 5-1/2" Paper Curling**
- **BEIGE** middle border - **TB65 - 3-1/2" Nordic Scroll**
- Flying geese units - echo in colors, stipple in **BEIGE**
- **BLACK** inner/middle borders - **TB67 - 1-1/2" Heart Chain**
- **RUST FLORAL** outer border - **TB43 - 7" Star Vine Border**

THIMBLEBERRIES quilt stencils by Quilting Creations International are available at your local quilt shop or visit www.quiltingcreations.com.

BINDING

Cutting
From **BLACK/BROWN** print:
- Cut 8, 2-3/4 x 44-inch strips
  Sew the binding to the quilt using a 3/8-inch seam allowance. This measurement will produce a 1/2-inch wide finished double binding. Refer to page 156 for **Binding** and **Diagonal Piecing** instructions.

Thimbleberries Celebration Sampler Quilt
64 x 82-inches

General Instructions

Getting Started

Yardage is based on 42-inch wide fabric. If your fabric is wider or narrower it will affect the amount of strips you need to cut in some patterns, and of course, it will affect the amount of fabric you have leftover. Generally, THIMBLEBERRIES patterns allow for a little extra fabric so you can confidently cut your pattern pieces with ease.

- A rotary cutter, mat, and wide clear plastic ruler with 1/8-inch markings are needed tools in attaining accuracy. A beginner needs good tools just as an experienced quiltmaker needs good equipment. A 24 x 36-inch mat board is a good size to own. It will easily accommodate the average quilt fabrics and will aid in accurate cutting. The plastic ruler you purchase should be at least 6 x 24-inches and easy to read. Do not purchase a smaller ruler to save money, the large size will be invaluable to your quiltmaking success.

- It is often recommended to prewash and press fabrics to test for colorfastness and possible shrinkage. If you choose to prewash, wash in cool water and dry in a cool to moderate dryer. Industry standards actually suggest that line drying is best. Shrinkage is generally very minimal and usually is not a concern. A good way to test your fabric for both shrinkage and colorfastness is to cut a 3-inch square of fabric. Soak the fabric in a white bowl filled with water. Squeeze the water out of the fabric and press it dry on a piece of muslin. If the fabric is going to release color it will do so either in the water or when it is pressed dry. Re-measure the 3-inch fabric square to see if it has changed size considerably (more than 1/4-inch). If it has, wash, dry, and press the entire yardage. This little test could save you hours in prewashing and pressing.

- Read instructions thoroughly before beginning a project. Each step will make more sense to you when you have a general overview of the whole process. Take one step at time and follow the illustrations. They will often make more sense to you than the words.

- For piecing, place right sides of the fabric pieces together and use 1/4-inch seam allowances throughout the entire quilt unless otherwise specifically stated in the directions. An accurate seam allowance is the most important part of the quiltmaking process after accurate cutting. All the directions are based on accurate 1/4-inch seam allowances. It is very important to check your sewing machine to see what position your fabric should be to get accurate seams. To test, use a piece of 1/4-inch graph paper, stitch along the quarter inch line as if the paper were fabric. Make note of where the edge of the paper lines up with your presser foot or where it lines up on the throat plate of your machine. Many quilters place a piece of masking tape on the throat plate to help guide the edge of the fabric. Now test your seam allowance on fabric. Cut 2, 2-1/2-inch squares, place right sides together and stitch along one edge. Press seam allowances in one direction and measure. At this point the unit should measure 2-1/2 x 4-1/2-inches. If it does not, adjust your stitching guidelines and test again. Seam allowances are included in the cutting sizes given in this book.

- Pressing is the third most important step in quiltmaking. As a general rule, you should never cross a stitched seam with another seam unless it has been pressed. Therefore, every time you stitch a seam it needs to be pressed before adding another piece. Often, it will feel like you press as much as you sew, and often that is true. It is very important that you press and not iron the seams. Pressing is a firm, up and down motion that will flatten the seams but not distort the piecing. Ironing is a back and forth motion and will stretch and distort the small pieces. Most quilters use steam to help the pressing process. The moisture does help and will not distort the shapes as long as the pressing motion is used.

- An old fashioned rule is to press seam allowances in one direction, toward the darker fabric. Often, background fabrics are light in color and pressing toward the darker fabric prevents the seam allowances from showing through to the right side. Pressing seam allowances in one direction is

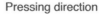
Pressing direction

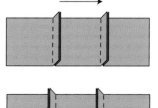

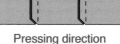
Pressing direction

thought to create a stronger seam. Also, for ease in hand-quilting, the quilting lines should fall on the side of the seam which is opposite the seam allowance. As you piece quilts, you will find these "rules" to be helpful but not necessarily always appropriate. Sometimes seams need to be pressed in the opposite direction so the seams of different units will fit together more easily which quilters refer to as seams "nesting" together. When sewing together two units with opposing seam allowances, use the tip of your seam ripper to gently guide the units under your presser foot. Sometimes it is necessary to re-press the seams to make the units fit together nicely. Always try to achieve the least bulk in one spot and accept that no matter which way you press, it may be a little tricky and it could be a little bulky.

Hints and Helps for Pressing Strip Sets

When sewing strips of fabric together for strip sets, it is important to press the seam allowances nice and flat, usually to the dark fabric. Be careful not to stretch as you press, causing a "rainbow effect." This will affect the accuracy and shape of the pieces cut from the strip set. Press on the wrong side first with the strips perpendicular to the ironing board. Flip the piece over and press on the right side to prevent little pleats from forming at the seams. Laying the strip set lengthwise on the ironing board seems to encourage the rainbow effect, as shown in diagram.

Avoid this "rainbow effect"

Trimming Side and Corner Triangles

Begin at a corner by lining up your ruler 1/4-inch beyond the points of the corners of the blocks as shown. Cut along the edge of the ruler. Repeat this procedure on all four sides of the quilt top.

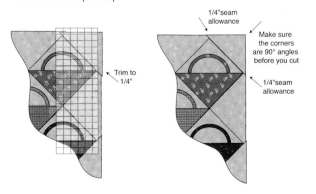

Trim to 1/4"

1/4"seam allowance

Make sure the corners are 90° angles before you cut

1/4"seam allowance

Borders

Step 1 With pins, mark the center points along all 4 sides of the quilt. For the top and bottom borders, measure the quilt from left to right through the middle. This measurement will give you the most accurate measurement that will result in a "square" quilt.

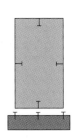

Step 2 Measure and mark the border lengths and center points on the strips cut for the borders before sewing them on.

Step 3 Pin the border strips to the quilt matching the pinned points on each of the borders and the quilt. Pin borders every 6 to 8-inches easing the fabric to fit as necessary. This will prevent the borders and quilt center from stretching while you are sewing them together. Stitch a 1/4-inch seam. Press the seam allowance toward the borders. Trim off excess border lengths.

Trim away excess fabric

Step 4 For the side borders, measure your quilt from top to bottom, including the borders just added, to determine the length of the side borders.

Step 5 Measure and mark the side border lengths as you did for the top and bottom borders.

Step 6 Pin and stitch the side border strips in place. When attaching the last two side outer border strips, taking a few backstitches at the beginning and the end of the border will help keep the quilt borders intact during the quilting process. Press and trim the border strips even with the borders just added.

Trim away excess fabric

Step 7 If your quilt has multiple borders, measure, mark, and sew additional borders to the quilt in the same manner.

Finishing the Quilt

Now that your quilt top is finished it needs to be layered with batting and backing, and prepared for quilting. Whether it is machine-quilted or hand-quilted, it is best to baste all 3 layers together. You may hand-baste with large basting stitches or pin-baste with medium size brass safety pins. Many quilters are satisfied with spray adhesives which are available at local quilt shops.

Step 1 Press the completed quilt top on the backside first, carefully clipping and removing hanging threads. Then press the quilt front making sure all seams are flat and all loose threads are removed.

Step 2 Remove the selvages from the backing fabric. Sew the long edges together; press. Trim the backing and batting so they are 4-inches larger than the quilt top.

Step 3 Mark the quilt top for quilting. Layer the backing, batting, and quilt top. Baste the 3 layers together and quilt. Work from the center of the quilt out to the edges. This will help keep the quilt flat by working the excess of the 3 layers to the outside edges.

Step 4 When quilting is complete, remove basting. Hand-baste the 3 layers together a scant 1/4-inch from the edge. This basting keeps the layers from shifting and prevents puckers from forming when adding the binding. Trim excess batting and backing fabric even with the edge of the quilt top.

Diagonal Piecing

Stitch diagonally   Trim to 1/4" seam allowance   Press seam open

Binding

The instructions for each quilt indicate the width to cut the binding used in that project. The measurements are sufficient for a quilt made of cotton fabrics and medium low loft quilt batting. If you use a high loft batt or combine a fluffy high loft batt with flannel fabrics, you may want to increase the width of the binding strips by adding 1/4 to 1/2-inch to the cut width of your binding. Always test a small segment of the binding before cutting all the strips needed.

Step 1 Diagonally piece the binding strips. Fold the strip in half lengthwise, wrong sides together; press.

Double-Layer Binding

Step 2 Unfold and trim one end at a 45° angle. Turn under the edge 1/4-inch; press. Refold the strip.

Fold Line

Step 3 With raw edges of the binding and quilt top even, stitch with a 3/8-inch seam allowance, unless otherwise specified, starting 2-inches from the angled end.

Step 4 Miter the binding at the corners. As you approach a corner of the quilt, stop sewing 3/8 to 1-inch from the corner of the quilt (use the same measurement as your seam allowance). Generally, a 3/8-inch seam allowance is used for regular cotton quilts and often a 1-inch seam allowance is used for flannel quilts. Each project in this book gives specific instructions for the binding width and seam allowance to be used.

3/8" to 1"   Binding Strip   Quilt Top

Step 5 Clip the threads and remove the quilt from under the presser foot.

Step 6 Flip the binding strip up and away from the quilt, then fold the binding down even with the raw edge of the quilt. Begin sewing at the upper edge. Miter all 4 corners in this manner.

Quilt Top   Quilt Top

Step 7 Trim the end of the binding so it can be tucked inside of the beginning binding about 1/2-inch. Finish stitching the seam.

Quilt Top   Quilt Top

Step 8 Turn the folded edge of the binding over the raw edges and to the back of the quilt so that the stitching line does not show. The corners will naturally turn with very little effort. Pin as needed to create a nice mitered corner on the back as well as on the front. Slip stitch the binding to the backside of the quilt by hand. To do this, slip your needle into the quilt back, sliding the needle approximately 1/4-inch. Bring it out of the fabric again and catch a few threads in the fold of the binding. At exactly the same point from which the needle emerged, insert it into the quilt back again, and take the next stitch. It is a good idea to take a double stitch approximately every 6 to 8-inches to anchor the binding.

Rotary Cutting

Safety First! The blades of a rotary cutter are very sharp and need to be for accurate cutting. Look at a variety of cutters to find one that feels good in your hand. All quality cutters have a safety mechanism to "close" the cutting blade when not in use. After each cut and before laying the rotary cutter down, close the blade. Soon this will become second nature to you and will prevent dangerous accidents. Always keep cutters out of the sight of children. Rotary cutters are very tempting to fiddle with when they are laying around. When your blade is dull or nicked, change it. Damaged blades do not cut accurately and require extra effort that can also result in slipping and injury. Also, always cut away from yourself for safety.

• Fold the fabric in half lengthwise matching the selvage edges.

• "Square off" the ends of your fabric before measuring and cutting pieces. This means that the cut edge of the fabric must be exactly perpendicular to the folded edge which creates a 90° angle. Align the folded and selvage

6" x 24" ruler

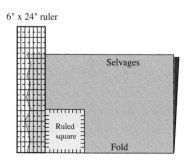

edges of the fabric with the lines on the cutting board, and place a ruled square on the fold. Place a 6 x 24-inch ruler against the side of the square to get a 90° angle. Hold the ruler in place, remove the square, and cut along the edge of the ruler. If you are left-handed, work from the other end of the fabric. Use the lines on your cutting board to help line up fabric, but not to measure and cut strips. Use a ruler for accurate cutting, always checking to make sure your fabric is lined up with horizontal and vertical lines on the ruler.

Cutting Side and Corner Triangles

In projects with side and corner triangles, the instructions have you cut side and corner triangles larger than needed. This will allow you to square up the quilt and eliminates the frustration of ending up with precut side and corner triangles that don't match the size of your pieced blocks.

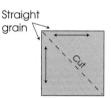

Corner Triangles

• To cut triangles, first cut squares. The project directions will tell you what size to make the squares and whether to cut them in half to make two triangles or to cut them in quarters to make four triangles, as shown in the diagrams. This cutting method will give you side triangles that have the straight of grain on the outside edges of the quilt. This is a very important part of quilt making that will help stabilize your quilt center.

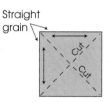

Side Triangles

Cutting Strips

When cutting strips or rectangles, cut on the crosswise grain. Strips can then be cut into squares or smaller rectangles.

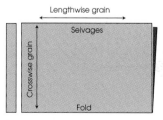

• If your strips are not straight after cutting a few of them, refold the fabric, align the folded and selvage edges with the lines on the cutting board, and "square off" the edge again by trimming to straighten, and begin cutting.

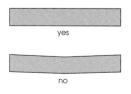

*The future belongs to those
who believe in the beauty
of their dreams.*

—Eleanor Roosevelt (1884–1962)
Former First Lady, writer and humanitarian

Project Index